VIBRATION COOKING

Vertamae Smart-Grosvenor

VIBRATION COOKING

OR

The Travel Notes of a Geechee Girl

The University of Georgia Press
ATHENS AND LONDON

A Sarah Mills Hodge Fund Publication

This publication is made possible in part through a grant from the Hodge
Foundation in memory of its founder, Sarah Mills Hodge, who devoted her life to
the relief and education of African Americans in Savannah, Georgia.

Published in 2011 by The University of Georgia Press
Athens, Georgia 30602
www.ugapress.org

Most University of Georgia Press titles are
available from popular e-book vendors.

Printed digitally

Library of Congress Cataloging-in-Publication Data

Smart-Grosvenor, Vertamae.
Vibration cooking, or, the travel notes of a Geechee girl /
Vertamae Smart-Grosvenor.
xxxix, 212 p. ; 22 cm.
"A Sarah Mills Hodge Fund publication."
Includes index.
ISBN-13: 978-0-8203-3739-5 (pbk. : alk. paper)
ISBN-10: 0-8203-3739-0 (pbk. : alk. paper)
1. African American cooking. 2. Cookery, American—Southern style.
3. African Amerians—Georgia—History. I. Title.
TX715.S638   2011
641.59'296073—dc22
2010027199

British Library Cataloging-in-Publication Data available

Originally published by Doubleday & Company, Inc.

dedicated to my mama and my grandmothers and my sisters in appreciation of the years that they worked in miss ann's kitchen and then came home to TCB in spite of slavery and oppression and the moynihan report.

*i noticed that all cookbooks have thanks and special thanks
to people who helped with the books. me too.

*i thank everyone who gave me recipes.

*i thank my editors marie dutton and loretta barrett.

*i thank len chandler for starting the whole johnson.

*i thank my testers mlles. kali and chandra because they HAD
to eat my cooking everyday.

*i thank felipe for burying rats in the garden.

*thanks to lucho for thanksgiving turkey.

*special thanks to richie havens, wilson pickett, johnny ace,
la lupe, john coltrane and miss billie holiday for singing and
playing everyday as i sat in my corner in the kitchen trying
to get my thing together.

*and to all my out to lunch friends who came to dinner, i want
to say thanks for coming
and for being beautiful

more

than

anything

walk through life
beautiful more than anything
stand in the sunlight
walk through life
love all the things that make you strong,
    be lovers,
        be anything
for all the people of
earth

imamu ameer baraka
(leroi jones)

Contents

Foreword

In Zora Neale Hurston's classic novel *Their Eyes Were Watching God*, Janie, the main character, recalls her past while sitting on the porch with her best friend, Pheoby. Hearing Janie's recollections of the times and people she'd known; advice she'd given and shared; and experiences she had of self-possession, determination, actualization, and growth, Pheoby declares breathlessly: "Ah done growed ten feet higher from jus' listenin' tuh you, Janie. Ah ain't satisfied wid mahself no mo'" (226).

Stories are like that. They hold our attention, filling our imagination by encouraging us to remember, even while they challenge us to expand our ways of thinking. The acts of telling, sharing, remembering, and listening to stories are often part and parcel of the lexicon of African American women's writings because storytelling has always been important in African American culture. Before and since leaving native shores, African American people sang, told, and chanted oral narratives concerning such things as nature and life, gods and heroes. It is the concept of the story and storytelling—varied, ambivalent, and contradictory, yet affirming—that defines Vertamae Smart-Grosvenor's *Vibration Cooking or The Travel Notes of a Geechee Girl*.

I was first introduced to Vertamae through her writing sometime in the mid-1990s. I was sitting on the plastic-covered sofa of
a family friend, and she was asking me about the directed course
of my all-important doctoral thesis. After much consternation
on my part, I said simply, "Food . . . black people and food."
In response, she pulled a book for me off her shelf. "Here," she
said, "then you need to read this." And she handed me a copy
of *Vibration Cooking*. Since that providential day, I have returned time and time again to Smart-Grosvenor's now classic
cookbook. The fact that *Vibration Cooking* is now in its fourth
reprinting bespeaks both its popularity and its necessity. The
current scholarly interest in women's studies, African American
studies, African diasporic studies, and food studies provides no
better time for reacquainting readers with Vertamae's work. Her
book is no less important now than when she first penned it over
forty years ago.

It is written that Vertamae was born and raised in the South
Carolina low country—in the village of Fairfax, Allendale
County, South Carolina. To be more (or less) exacting, she "was
born across the branch from where Uncle Bubba lives now"
(*Vibration* 3) in 1938. So begins the narrative cookbook that is
a combination of fact, fiction, folktale, poetry, drama, and culinary anthropology. It is this arrangement that originally struck
me. First glance revealed that Vertamae's writing style gave way
to more stories than recipes. Or as literary scholar Doris Witt
describes it, "[R]ecipe gives rise to anecdote, and anecdote to
recipe" (156). The cookbook was unlike any I had ever seen. This
was so much the case that initially I put it down and decided that
while it was a nice gift, it did not fit the kind of research I had
in mind on African American foodways. Years later, however,
I would return to Smart-Grosvenor's work for what it revealed
about women who use food to build better lives for themselves
and their families. In *Building Houses out of Chicken Legs: Black
Women, Food, and Power*, I analyze the cultural uses of chicken

and other fare to examine, acknowledge, and give voice to black women who "shap[e] vital aspects of their lives with food" (1). Women like Vertamae, who are culinary foremothers, detail in various ways "a feminist consciousness of community building, cultural work, and personal identity." Over time the work they create serves as a tool of "self-expression, actualization, resistance, accommodation, and power" (Williams-Forson 1–2). Vertamae's self-ethnography celebrates black mothers and daughters who practice cooking both as an art form and as a demonstration of self-reliance. We read about these women, use their recipes, and even listen to their voices. I am not convinced, however, that we actually "hear" or listen to what they say, especially when it is delivered in a way that defies what is expected.

Society perpetually ignores the stories told by and about black women, resulting in a continuous need for projects of reclamation. Beginning in earnest with the 1960s and 1970s, black women have been central to these recovery activities. Consider, for example, where we would be without that first generation of black female academics who gave us the literary criticism and anthologies on other black women writers—past and present—who now compose the historiography of black feminist literary writing, or where we would be without the Schomburg Center's collaboration with Henry Louis Gates and Oxford University Press that resulted in the thirty-volume Schomburg Library of Nineteenth-Century Black Women Writers collection. This project brought to the fore the foundation of the African American and women's literary traditions, republishing the first book of poetry by an African American (Phillis Wheatley); the first book of essays (Ann Plato); and the first novel published by a black person in the United States (*Our Nig*, by Harriet Wilson [1859]). And over twenty years later we are still recovering black women's literary traditions—this time in the culinary world.

By no means is *Vibration Cooking* the first cookbook by an African American woman. Culinary historians long ago established that former slave Abby Fisher recorded her recipes as early as 1881. But a recovery process is still in the works. In the wake of many unknown cookbooks authored by African Americans few stand venerable and still in print—Edna Lewis's compendiums on southern food and Jessica Harris's critically acclaimed cookbooks documenting the foods and foodways of the African diaspora are among the few.

Yet we are now in a moment of African American culinary efflorescence, with recent cookbooks acknowledging African American celebrities (Patti LaBelle), lifeways (*Real Men Can Cook*), and health disparities (diabetes, cancer) pervading bookstore shelves. Adding to the works in the popular press are those produced in the last two decades by and about African American foodways from a scholarly point of view. These include Doris Witt's *Black Hunger*, Andrew Warnes's *Hunger Overcome*, my own *Building Houses out of Chicken Legs*, Anne L. Bower's *African American Foodways*, Frederick Douglass Opie's *Hog and Hominy*, and A. Breeze Harper's *Sistah Vegan*. But there must be more and there needs to be more. Reprinting Vertamae's *Vibration Cooking or The Travel Notes of a Geechee Girl* is part of this process.

Originally published in 1970, the cookbook is often referred to as an "underground classic" for being among the first to expose readers to low-country cuisine with ingredients that include seafood such as shrimp, oysters, and crab, as well as products from the soil such as greens and sweet potatoes and, of course, rice. From this vantage point, it is a "normal" cookbook, a "kitchen bible" of sorts. But when compared with other cookbooks—both of the period and generally—Vertamae's cookbook is distinctive. It is not a book filled with straightforward instruction on how to cook a selection of entrées. It does not necessarily guide and direct a person in making particular culinary treats. To be sure, its value does lie in its suggested culinary offerings—tasty and mouthwatering, if not at times eccentric (with recipe names like

"Nat Turner Apple Pork Thing"). But through cooking notes and quips about life experiences Vertamae also illustrates with lyrical liveliness the beauty of black identities: "Salad Niçoise is a French name but just like with anything else when soul folks get it they take it out into another thing" (60). More to the point, she exercises verbal acuity about food in the course of sharing her social exchanges, her social circles, and her social universe. She is unconcerned with measurements, giving us license to "do your thing your way." She writes: "And when I cook, I never measure or weigh anything. I cook by vibration. I can tell by the look and smell of it. Most of the ingredients in this book are approximate. Some of the recipes that people gave me list the amounts, but for my part, I just do it by vibration. Different strokes for different folks. Do your thing your way" (xxxvii). Such is the nature of cooking by "vibration." With this, we enter Vertamae's world— a world of inconsistencies, a world full of exploration, experimentation, and fiction. In essence, she invites us to experience her world and walk away with different interpretations of that encounter.

To hear and read "fully" what women like Vertamae are saying in their cookbooks, Anne Bower, author of *Recipes for Reading*, suggests that we have to "know what they read, where they had lived, what they might have aspired to." The more we read the more that is unveiled as "part collective autobiography, part history, part fiction" (3). These unveiled stories, Bower goes on to explain, reveal values, innovation, style, and, more importantly perhaps, cultural work. Cookbooks tell us much about the lives of women, and through the words of such women we find their "personal, family, and cultural drama[s]" (Theophano 1). In this way, Vertamae's is a classic cookbook. Yet in the manner in which Vertamae wrote *Vibration Cooking*, she also anticipated the need to avoid what Nigerian novelist Chimamanda Adichie calls "the single story." In short, the single story is the one that popular culture has delivered time and time again. It is the story that places people—particularly those considered "other"—in a box that is manageable and relatively comprehensible. It is the default place in which the speaker, writer, performer, and activist must remain so that sense can be made of them. It does not allow for, yield to, or welcome the creative consciousness or, as Barbara Christian argues, any attempt "to use the range of one's voice, to attempt to express the totality of self" (234).

Anne Goldman, Quandra Prettyman, Rafia Zafar, and Doris Witt are among those who have read Vertamae's text "fully," and they have written extensively and insightfully about it— arguments and observations that do not need to be rehashed here. They each, in one way or another, link Vertamae's style and thinking to Zora Neale Hurston. Such should come as no surprise because Vertamae has said as much herself. Asked to list five famous people (living or dead) that she would invite to a dinner party, for her public radio profile for "Just the Facts," Vertamae headed her list with Hurston. Helping to round out her guest list were Sun Ra and Gabriel García Márquez. Given this, it is hardly surprising that fictional journalism, cosmology, riffing, razzing, sassy talk, and tricksterlike language pervade her auto-ethnography. Alice Walker's observation about the spiritual friend she reclaimed is equally warranted here: "I think we are better off if we think of Zora Neale Hurston as an artist, period— rather than as the artist/politician most black writers have been required to be. This frees us to appreciate the complexity and richness of her work in the same way we can appreciate Billie Holiday's glorious phrasing or Bessie Smith's perfect and raunchy lyrics, without the necessity of ridiculing the former's addiction to heroin or the latter's excessive love of gin" (3). Taking this suggestion, I want to stake out a position about Vertamae's seminal work that I think bears considering: part of what makes Vertamae's cookbook a manifesto is the way in which she intervenes in the dialogues—then and now—to resituate the place and the definitions of African American food and foodways and the roles of the black women who procure, prepare, present, and consume them. We accept this along with the inconsistencies and contradictions in the text as her artistry.

In most of her writings, including *Vibration Cooking* and *Thursdays and Every Other Sunday Off: A Domestic Rap by Verta Mae*, the influences of the era of new black consciousness and of the Black Arts Movement are ever present. From the opening poem borrowed from Amiri Baraka / LeRoi Jones's short story "Answers in Progress," we know (if we do the research and "read fully") that Vertamae is riffing off Baraka's style and form. Vertamae's use of the short poem situated in the middle of Baraka's narrative, however, bears further explanation. Though seemingly just another opening epigraph, the poem's strategic placement at the beginning of Vertamae's text is structurally crucial because it signals that this book is going to disrupt the cookbook genre.

In his analysis of Baraka's "Answers in Progress," Jürgen Grandt illustrates the central importance and usefulness of the short story and its embedded poem to *Vibration Cooking*. Baraka's story "Answers in Progress" is about space aliens converging on New Jersey in 1967 during the ebb of a black uprising against the white political system. Though fictional, it predicted the real rebellions that would take place months later in Newark. After a brief introduction to the melee, the story abruptly begins: "The next day the spaceships landed. Art Blakey records was what they were looking for" ("Answers" 219). Baraka's early focus in this story on the jazz bebop great should not be overlooked. During the 1960s Baraka leaned toward bebop and then the free jazz movement, an improvisational and experimental form rooted in chaotic blends of blues and gospel. Baraka drew on these jazz traditions to expand the black literary tradition. Grandt suggests that both in its tone and in its narrative the short story reflects this intention in that it "departs deliberately from the conventions of storytelling . . . in a style that revolts against conventional prose"

(4). Baraka juxtaposes the frenzy of the writing, however, with a utopian vision of a harmonious future that imagines the emergence of a new black race. Grandt writes "like a snapshot—or sound clip—of the prolonged uprising, the story mixes prose, shaped poetry and song, lacks any exposition or closure, and is generally allusive rather than descriptive. . . . It also draws on several different genres and artistic movements; most notably, of course, it parodies the science fiction genre" (70). From Baraka's point of view, the short story is about value and placing value on a black aesthetic. But more than this it is about personal transformation (by the time it was written LeRoi Jones had become Amiri Baraka) and new black identities in new spaces. Black music and its liberatory possibilities disrupt the spaces of white domination, making way for the new utopia.

The poem that Vertamae uses to open her book has been described as a narrative disruption in "Answers in Progress." Hardly revolutionary in its admonishment, the stanza used by Vertamae speaks of aesthetic beauty even as it speaks of sustaining life:

> walk through life
> beautiful more than anything
> stand in the sunlight
> walk through life
> love all the things that make you strong,
>   be lovers,
>   be anything
> for all the people of
> earth

Vertamae signifies on the jazz poetics of Baraka and the Afro-cosmology of Sun Ra in that she too references personal transformation and black identities in new and different spaces. But she also writes about the beauty of improvisation and self-definition—through food. While music ruptures and reconfigures the social spaces of white domination for Baraka, food and the culinary arts perform this task for Vertamae. Although Vertamae did not have the benefit of these analyses when she borrowed the poem, she was nonetheless aware of its meaning in the circles of her time. Anticipating Grandt, Vertamae's narrative avails itself of the characteristics of jazz music by incorporating as much ambiguity and convolution as clarity. It was revolutionary—or intended to be. This disruptive style, then, became the vehicle through which Vertamae staged her own futuristic envisioning of black America. But she did it using the tools of her talent—food and the gustatory arts. She elevated this form of African American style and folkways to a place of recognition—one that exceeded consumption. Soul food particularly, along with the problematic concepts connected to it, was but one of the spaces of this culinary disruption.

Written in response to the statement that African Americans had no distinctive foodways patterns, Amiri Baraka in his collection of essays *Home* describes most of what we know today as food eaten by people (collectively) in the South. Among these foods are grits, hoppin' John (black-eyed peas and rice), fried fish and chicken, buttermilk biscuits, dumplings, lima beans, corn, string beans, okra, smoky or hot barbecue, and most anything coming from the pig, including neck bones and pork chops. Sweet tea or lemonade and a large wedge of sweet-potato pie round out the description. To be sure, most any cookbook on southern foods will boast the same (or a similar) lineup of foods, but in the 1960s these foods were representative of blackness as many migrants from the South still ate them. Forty years later the phrase is as contested as it was back then, but it serves the purpose of locating in a particular time, place, and consciousness people who identified with and participated in a struggle for liberation. Often this struggle, like others, took the form of a rebuttal. Baraka, for example, issued his comments on "Soul Food" to refute the beliefs of a young black man who wrote in *Esquire* that African Americans had neither a characteristic language nor cuisine. Similarly, Vertamae wrote a letter to the editor of *Time* magazine in response to the author of "Food: Eating Like Soul Brothers," who essentially eschewed soul food, describing it as "fatty, overcooked and underseasoned." For chitlins, the "true 'stone soul' dish," he assigned the descriptor "football bladder," summing up his diatribe by dismissing soul food as a tasteless cuisine whose popularity is simply "a fad." Compelled to respond, Vertamae wrote:

> Sirs:
> You have the bad taste to say that soul food is tasteless. Your taste buds are so racist that they can't even deal with black food. Your comment that the "soul food fad" is going to be short-lived is dumb. But then your whole culture is made of short-lived fads. So you white folks just keep on eating that white foam rubber bread that sticks to the roof of your mouth, and keep on eating Minute Rice and instant potatoes, instant cereals and drinking instant milk and stick to your instant culture. And I will stick to the short-lived fad that brought my ancestors through four hundred years of oppression. (175)

Vertamae reprints this refutation in *Vibration Cooking* in the context of girlfriend talk with her friend Stella. "*Time* magazine couldn't take any more," however, as Vertamae explains, so she goes on to tell Stella how the letter would have continued: "Soul food is more than chitlins and collard greens, ham hocks and black-eyed peas. . . . [It] is about a people who have a lot of heart and soul." Vertamae then tells Stella to "[a]sk Doctor Christiaan Barnard about them black hearts" (175). This last line is characteristic Vertamae, with its reference to the South African heart surgeon Christiaan Barnard, who despite great opposition during apartheid performed kidney and heart transplants on colored children—a testament to her transnational awareness and the plight of African peoples around the world. Doris Witt offers another explanation: "Grosvenor's treatment of the late 1960s popularity of soul food needs to be understood, then, in conjunction with her more encompassing critique of how racial boundaries are used by members of the dominant classes to consolidate and perpetuate their power. She foregrounds the hypocrisy of a system which constructs racial boundaries so as to ensure that the dominant group will have power to determine the circumstances under which those boundaries will be crossed, as inevitably they are" (160).

In other words, white people criticize foods like chitlins as tasteless until those same people decide that they are not and are, instead, a delicacy. Take, for instance, the time that Vertamae goes to a "fancy" Paris restaurant with a few people—the kind "usually found in Chinese restaurants." Excitedly, they offer to order for her. She writes, "So these people order for me and they are just on pins and needles, dying, really dying for me to taste this enjoyable rare dish. Well thank you Jesus the food arrives and it ain't nothing but CHITTERLINGS in the form of a sausage. They call it *andouillette*" (original emphasis; 93). This tongue-in-cheek illustration of culinary tourism—the intentional, exploratory participation in the foodways of other cultures—further exposes the hypocrisy associated with crossing social and racial boundaries. Chitterlings are tasteless to some whites until they are labeled "andouillette," then they represent gastronomic refinement. Similar is Vertamae's play on the term "black hearts." Hearts are, of course, part of the human anatomy as well as part of the food chain. Playing off both of those meanings in the context of racism and apartheid, black hearts become parts (food/people) that are not to be saved until one member of the "dominant class" decides that such is okay. Then, of course, Vertamae implies, it is perfectly acceptable.

During the era of the Black Arts Movement the ideals of black solidarity were emblazoned in almost every form of cultural outlay. According to Askia Touré, the movement "was composed of poets, dramatists, visual artists, film-makers, [and] musicians, led by a dedicated Cadre of Maroon visionaries who wrote a new chapter in African American history with the development of an ethnic-based Aesthetic." Notice, however, the lack of mention of anyone or anything directly connected to the culinary arts. This is likely one reason Vertamae's work was relatively effaced by those in her set when it first appeared in the 1970s. Like most studies of food at the time it was probably seen as unworthy of serious attention. In the raging war of high and low culture, cookbooks—dismissed as largely women's domestic fare—were not elevated.

At a time when women were seeking acceptance to an admittedly sexist social justice movement, they nonetheless continued to write with a heightened focus on the liberation struggles of pan-African people. Poems like Nikki Giovanni's "Nigger Can You Kill?" was important as much for its subject matter as for its tone—radical, strident, controversial. Recognizing this and the fact that some of what was being spouted was actually rhetoric without action, Vertamae slips in a dig when she talks about her friend, the revolutionary, who comes to visit. While at her house he spots a mouse in the bathroom. Amid Vertamae's admonition to "[k]ill him, kill him," he retreats with pleas to call the fire department. To this Vertamae threatens, "[I]f he didn't kill the mouse and flush him down the toilet I would tell everyone that he was going to kill white folks but was afraid of mice" (72). Eventually her friend does the deed, prompting Vertamae to note in her book, "Just goes to show you everybody talking about revolution ain't making it" (73).

Riffing off the familiar "Everybody Talkin' 'bout Heaven Ain't Going There," Vertamae's act of "crackin', but fackin'" is indicative of one of the many clever ways that African Americans engage in ridiculing their oppressors and waging forms of verbal resistance. It is part of the "spoken virtuosity" found in the dozens, in signifying, in folktales, in sermons, and of course, in rap.

When Vertamae writes on "Soul Food" in *McCall's* magazine, with its focus on a decidedly white female audience, and argues that "soul food ain't frozen collard green," but it is "vanilla wafers," she is, like her contemporaries at that time, conveying in written form the many performances of black speech and music. Like her foremother Zora Neale Hurston, Vertamae employs various genres, through eclecticism and the use of montage, to explore numerous possibilities, and in doing so she defies and resists categorization and definition. She mines black folklore and its tales to wage her personal war for expanding black space and place. She shrugs off the encumbrances of political messages to embrace necessary ambivalence, being noncommittal at times because it would limit her portrayals of and connections to black life through food. In stretching the boundaries of the language of food she reveals its complexities even as she works with its ubiquity. That she does this while refusing to compromise her crafts—plural—perhaps makes people uncomfortable, then and now. Though she insists on the importance of black women being seen as more than domestics and certainly as more than the limited representations prevailing at the time, she apparently did not fit in with "the struggle."

But this is not to say that Vertamae was an unknown and her work not read. Undoubtedly, plenty of folks "down home" heard that Vertamae had a book out, and they read it just to see what was in there. When Alice Walker came upon Hurston's *Mules and Men*, she shared it with her relatives, and they found in the book elements of their southern roots. Likewise, in the case of Vertamae, we know at least one other southerner had the book on her shelf, which is how I came into its possession. So even when Vertamae's books have been out of print and/or when the larger public arena has not necessarily offered accolades, her books have still been read, referred to, and possibly revered among certain communities of people. This is not surprising. What should come as a surprise is that more black women have not been acknowledged for the cultural agency they exhibited with food—through cookbook writing—during the late 1960s and the 1970s. With the exception of one or two singular recipe collections and authors, the corpus of African American culinary print history from bygone eras is largely only reflected in an appendix. At a time when many black women were working with food in and out of the homes of white folks, Vertamae was offering up a gendered critique to this and other experiences that sought to commodify black culinary arts.

There is, then, a *power* in exploding the single story. Chimamanda Adichie says, "Power is the ability not just to tell the story of another person, but to make it the definitive story of that person. The Palestinian poet Mourid Barghouti writes that if you want to dispossess a people, the simplest way to do it is to tell their story, and to start with, 'secondly.' Start the story with the arrows of the Native Americans, and not with the arrival of the British, and you have an entirely different story. Start the story with the failure of the African state, and not with the colonial creation of the African state, and you have an entirely different story." Start the story with misperceptions of African American food and foodways, and not with a black woman's perspective, and you have an entirely different story. These changes to the familiar story, it seems, are part of the power of *Vibration Cooking*. The book, in all of its facets, with its disruptions and ambiguities, forces the reader to be confused, thrilled, excited, and dismayed by various experiences of African American life. In sharing her life stories—fact and fiction—Vertamae debunks the belief that there is a single story about black life. Even if she has to create the experiences in her imagination, the fact remains that she presents different versions of multiple stories—hers and others.

In sharing the stories of her travels and the foods she encounters, Vertamae discredits the notion that black people *only* eat fried chicken, chitlins, collard greens, and other southern foods that we see directly reflecting particular geographical locations and migratory patterns. To be sure, as she says, black people also have their "get down foods." However, such cuisine does not forge the totality of black food habit. Rather, food is food—it is sexy, it is personal, it is feminine and masculine, it is good, bad, et cetera. Writing during the pinnacle of the Black Power movement, Vertamae asserts not only that "Black is Beautiful" but also that Black is . . . ! Black food is more than kitchen scraps; black women are more than mammy figures, and black culture is more than a monolith. Vertamae may have distanced herself from the highly contentious phrase "soul food," but she still includes discussions of chitlins, collard greens, fried chicken, and hoppin' John; however, she also includes eggplant, artichokes, and Irish potato soup. For Vertamae all such foods are part of a black diner's soul collective. And why not? Vertamae has always postulated that we need to consider the range of foods in the African American culinary repertoire. As she says—soul is in you, not in the food! So when substitutions must be made, then so be it: "Millie came from Germany one year. She arrived just in time for the black-eyes and rice. And that year I cooked the peas with beef neck bones instead of swine cause so many brothers and sisters had given up swine. I had ham hocks on the side for others" (xxxix).

I *like* this book! A woman after my own heart, Vertamae says that she never measures or weighs anything—validation of my own cooking style. I can rarely give you a recipe because each time I cook—greens, leeks, chicken, whatever—I put whatever I feel like putting in. I have always cooked by vibration, but until I read Vertamae's book, I had no name for it!

I like the fact that Vertamae claims her manuscript was "discovered" only after her daughter Kali's poetry book was accepted for publication. I like that she is not concerned about us knowing the particulars of her private life (real or imagined) and feels compelled to talk about cooking, cleaning, and the joys (and lows) of motherhood: "I found it [the apartment] on April 4 (my birthday) and it was on the Rue des Ursulines (Chandra's middle name is Ursule) and we found a hanger in the closet that said Grosvenor House. I thought that was too much for me so I took it. The kitchen was very tiny but I bammed a bunch of nails in the wall and unpacked my trunkful of kitchen stuff and set in to try my hand at 'stewed Jerusalem artichokes'" (63). I like that the recipes range from realistic (Ambrosia, Souse, Fish Head Stew) to the absurd (Betty's Barbecued Gator Tails).

I like too that she includes a chapter on African clothes, where she connects foods to their ancestry and justifies her desire to wear African garb by stating that "if squash and a potato and a duck and a pepper can grow and look like their ancestors, I know damn well that I can walk around dressed like mine" (118).

I like that at a time of heightened feminism, Vertamae sharply asserts her love for men who enjoy food (xxxviii), keenly linking the pleasures of the body and bearing out this assertion by Anne Bower: "In gaining academic acceptance, earlier feminists often felt compelled to repress expressions of interests in domestic life for fear that such expression would consign them to an essential-ized 'feminine' role. Nowadays, feminists (female and male!) col-lectively have the assurance and breadth to allow us to seek our history, traditions, and voices in the kitchen. . . . [W]omen's tradi-tional lives [now] are worth thinking about, worth writing about, worth reading" (*Recipes* 9). Vertamae rightly foresees such a fu-ture for black women.

I like especially that Vertamae "talks back" to her foremothers and paves the way for her literary daughters by using the episto-lary form to talk to her "friend" Stella about food, sex, and love:

Stella,
    You want to know why I say soul food is life? Well, first off, food ain't nothing but food. No matter who you are and where you live you got to eat. Cooking is a creative thing. Cooking is one of the highest of all the arts. It can make or

break life. . . . So, if you cook with love and feed people, you got two forces cooled out already. Dig, food can cause happiness or unhappiness, health or sickness and make or break marriages.

. . . [S]oul food depends on what you put in it. I don't mean spices either.

If you have a serious, loving, creative energetic attitude towards life, when you cook, you cook with the same attitude. (170–71)

Most of all, I like that she is as inconsistent as she wants to be with her vibes, her experiences, and the stories she tells, ending her book with the promise "To Be Continued." This lets us know that while she certainly has come into a particular woman-consciousness, she is ever always in a state of growth and becoming. This may be Vertamae's version of the female *Sweet Sweetback's Baadasssss Song*—the picaresque story of an African American man on his flight from white authority stirring up trouble but leaving those excited who have come in contact with him. Rather than fleeing, Vertamae confronts the establishment head-on and is herself regardless of the time and the place. Rather than limit herself to being a writer, commentator, performer, mother, culinary artist, or friend—she is all of these things at once and in contradiction.

We have come a long way since needing to justify the usefulness of cookbooks as more than a container for recipes. And one would think that we are coming to a place where we no longer have to explain the "vibrations" of African American cuisine. Certainly by now we know of the many culinary contributions made by African American women in preparing food and in caring for their families, friends, and communities. In coming full circle with another reprinting of *Vibration Cooking* I hope that we are getting to a point where we no longer need to be reminded of the intersections between food, culture, gender, race, and politics.

My 1970s version of *Vibration Cooking* is highly stained but intact. It still bears the price of $1.95 and the torn Crisco recipes for "Quick 'n' easy salmon patties" and "nine-inch single pie crusts," identifying the proclivities of its previous owner. But the marginalia, the sticky notes, and dog-ear corners are all mine, joining past and present—demonstrating the relevance of *Vibration Cooking* today as much as yesterday. Each time I read it now, I put it down with a sigh and think to myself, Ah done growed ten feet higher from jus' readin' 'bout you . . . Vertamae.

Psyche Williams-Forson
University of Maryland College Park

WORKS CITED

Adichie, Chimamanda. "The Danger of a Single Story." TEDGlobal 2009 Conference, Oxford, UK, 21–24 July 2009. Online audio clip. TEDGlobal2009. Accessed on 24 November 2009. http://www.ted.com/talks/chimamanda_adichie_the_danger_of_a_single_story.html.

Baraka, Amiri (LeRoi Jones). "Answers in Progress." *The Fiction of LeRoi Jones / Amiri Baraka*. Chicago: Lawrence Hill Books, 2000. 219–22.

———. *Blues People: Negro Music in White America*. New York: William Morrow, 1963.

———. *Home: Social Essays*. New York: William Morrow, 1966.

Bower, Anne L., ed. *African American Foodways: Explorations of History and Culture*. Champaign: University of Illinois Press, 2007.

———. *Recipes for Reading: Community Cookbooks, Stories, Histories*. Amherst: University of Massachusetts Press, 1997.

Christian, Barbara. "Trajectories of Self-Definition: Placing Contemporary Afro-American Women's Fiction." *Conjuring: Black Women, Fiction, and Literary Tradition*. Ed. Hortense Spillers and Marjorie Pryse. Bloomington: Indiana University Press,1985. 234–48.

"Food: Eating Like Soul Brothers." *Time* 24 January 1969.

Giovanni, Nikki. *Black Feeling, Black Talk/Black Judgment*. New York: Perennial, 1971.

Goldman, Anne. "'I Yam What I Yam': Cooking, Culture, and Colonialism." *De/Colonizing the Subject: The Politics of Gender in Women's Autobiography*. Ed. Sidonie Smith and Julia Watson. Minneapolis: University of Minnesota Press, 1992. 169–95.

Grandt, Jürgen E. *Kinds of Blue: The Jazz Aesthetic in African American Narrative*. Columbus: Ohio State University Press, 2005.

Harper, A. Breeze, ed. *Sistah Vegan: Black Female Vegans Speak on Food, Identity, Health, and Society*. New York: Lantern Books, 2010.

Hurston, Zora Neale. *Their Eyes Were Watching God*. Urbana: University of Illinois Press, 1978.

Opie, Frederick Douglass. *Hog and Hominy: Soul Food from Africa to America*. New York: Columbia University Press, 2008.

Prettyman, Quandra. "Come Eat at My Table: Lives with Recipes." *Southern Quarterly* 30.1–2 (1992): 131–40.

Smart-Grosvenor, Vertamae [Verta Mae; Vertamae Smart Grosvenor]. "Soul Food." *McCall's* Sept. 1970: 72–75.

———. *Thursdays and Every Other Sunday Off: A Domestic Rap by Verta Mae*. Garden City, N.Y.: Doubleday, 1972.

———. *Vibration Cooking or The Travel Notes of a Geechee Girl*. Garden City, N.Y.: Doubleday, 1970. Athens: University of Georgia Press, 2011.

Sweet Sweetback's Baadasssss Song. Dir. Melvin Van Peebles. 1971. DVD. Cinemation Industries, 2003.

Theophano, Janet. *Eat My Words: Reading Women's Lives through the Cookbooks They Wrote*. New York: Palgrave Macmillan, 2003.

Touré, Askia. "The Official Website of Askia Toure." 2004. Accessed July 24, 2009. http://www.askiatoure.com/.

Walker, Alice. "Dedication—On Refusing to Be Humbled by Second Place in a Contest You Did Not Design: A Tradition by Now." *I Love Myself When I Am Laughing . . . And Then Again: A Zora Neale Hurston Reader*, ed. Alice Walker. New York: Feminist Press at CUNY, 1979. 1–5.

Warnes, Andrew. *Hunger Overcome: Food and Resistance in Twentieth Century African American Life*. Athens: University of Georgia Press, 2004.

Williams-Forson, Psyche. *Building Houses out of Chicken Legs: Black Women, Food, and Power*. Chapel Hill: University of North Carolina Press, 2006.

Witt, Doris. *Black Hunger: Food and the Politics of U.S. Identity*. New York: Oxford University Press, 1999. Minneapolis: University of Minnesota Press, 2004.

Zafar, Rafia. "The Signifying Dish: Autobiography and History in Two Black Women's Cookbooks." *Feminist Studies* 25.2 (1999): 449–70.

Preface to the 2011 Edition

Dear Reader:

Thank you for reading *Vibration Cooking*. It is not, as some have suggested, a work of fiction. I *was* a three-pound premature twin. My brother weighed six pounds and didn't make it. It is true that they said, "The boy done dead and the gal ain't gonna make it." It is true Grandmamma Sula said, "O yes she will!" and ordered them to go milk the goat and fetch an eyedropper and shoe box. She fed me the milk with the eyedropper, swaddled me in a blanket, opened the oven door of the stove, placed the shoe box on the door. And I'm here to tell you that story and all the others in the book are what the devil do despise. The natural truth!

People ask me how I came to write the book. The book happened because I wanted to creatively express myself. As a child in Carolina I loved to recite poems and "act out scenes." When we moved to Philadelphia, I was in all the church pageants and school plays. At home I wrote my own and played all the parts. I wanted to be an actress. At fifteen I began studying with Jaspher Deeter at the legendary Hedgerow Theater. I knew it was rough out there for black actresses, but that didn't stop me from studying. Jaspher said I was good actress, so I continued to study, joined a little theatre group in Philadelphia, and was cast in several productions. When I first got to Paris, I read that an American "little theater" was casting for a play and went to audition but was told that I was not suited for any part. Years later I saw the director at a party in New York. . . . He said he meant that I hadn't been right for that play and I should have come back again. Yeah, right.

In the late 1960s I was living on the Lower East Side of New York. My creative urge was still with me, but taking classes cost money, then more because I had to pay a babysitter too. I had two children and less money. I kept asking myself what I could do to express myself. Writing seemed the answer. I borrowed a typewriter from my neighbor.

What could I write about? Don't they say write about what you know? Well, raised on a farm, I knew about food, so I decided, "A Cookbook!" I wanted to do a different kind of cookbook. And I did. I never imagined the experiences and places this book would take me or the people I would meet. I knew that having a book published, doing TV and radio interviews, even films, would change my life, but I never imagined how *for real* it would change my life.

Back in the day, a cookbook had about a page and a half of introduction, recipes, and no narrative. Coming from a culture of storytellers, I wanted to tell stories about the gatherings, the people, the food, and the history of the food. For decades the history of African American food was mucked up. "Soul food," aka black folks' eats, was said to have developed out of master's leftovers. It was said that slaves brought okra. Watermelon. They carried benne seeds over in their ears. Did they pick up their watermelons at the baggage claim?

Education is the key.

In one of the *America's Family Kitchen* shows I did for PBS, I talked about South Carolina low country and how we call peanuts goobers, okra gombo, and eggplant Guinea Squash. Boston PBS was flooded with calls and letters from people who assumed that I was making a slur against Italians. I went to *Webster's Dictionary* and photocopied the page of entries for Guinea, and then I photocopied a map with the country on it and sent it to the station in case they wanted to respond to people.

Now, forty years later, after the birth of my baby *Vibration Cooking*, we've changed, but some people still carry culinary baggage, carry their associations and sensitivities about food still too close.

Food is not racial. Let it go. Jettison the baggage. Appreciate and Enjoy.

Cook!

Eat!

March 26, 2010

The Demystification of Food

In reading lots and lots of cookbooks written by white folks it occurred to me that people very casually say Spanish rice, French fries, Italian spaghetti, Chinese cabbage, Mexican beans, Swedish meatballs, Danish pastry, English muffins and Swiss cheese. And with the exception of black bottom pie and niggertoes, there is no reference to black people's contribution to the culinary arts. White folks act like they invented food and like there is some weird mystique surrounding it— something that only Julia and Jim can get to. There is no mystique. Food is food. Everybody eats!

And when I cook, I never measure or weigh anything. I cook by vibration. I can tell by the look and smell of it. Most of the ingredients in this book are approximate. Some of the recipes that people gave me list the amounts, but for my part, I just do it by vibration. Different strokes for different folks. Do your thing your way.

The amount of salt and pepper you want to use is your business. I don't like to get in people's business. I have made everything in here and found everything to be everything and everything came out very together. If you have any trouble, I would suggest that you check out your kitchen vibrations. *What kind of pots are you using?* Throw out all of them except the black ones. The cast-iron ones like your mother used to use. Can't no Teflon fry no fried chicken. I only use black pots and brown earthenware in the kitchen. White enamel is not what's happening.

I don't like fancy food. I like simple—plain—ordinary—call it what you choose. I like what is readily available. It is very easy to do special things. Like a cake you only make on your first cousin by your mother's second marriage's birthday. Or a ham you make for Sam's wedding anniversary every other February 29. I'm talking about being able to turn the daily ritual of cooking for your family into a beautiful everyday happening. Now, that's something else again.

The supermarket is full of exciting and interesting food. It don't really matter where you live. After a minute, there ain't but so many ways you can cook a sweet potato. I remember at a market on Rue Monge in Paris I saw some potatoes that looked very much in the sweet potato family. I asked and the lady said, *"C'est le pomme de terre douce."* She said that they came from Madagascar. Just then a sister from Senegal came by. I asked her how they cooked them where she came from and she said, "We make tarts . . ." (nothing but sweet potato pie); "We fry them in butter and sugar . . ." (nothing but candied sweet potatoes); "We roast them in the oven . . ." (nothing but baked sweet potatoes). It don't matter if it's Dakar or Savannah, you can cook exotic food any time you want. Just turn on the imagination, be willing to change your style and let a little soul food in. Ayischia says you are what you eat and that's what I believe, too.

An evening with good food and good vibrations from the people with whom you're eating—that's the kind of evening that turns me on. I like men who enjoy food. Cooking for a man is a very feminine thing, and I can't understand how a woman can feed her man TV dinners. Food is sexy and you can tell a lot about people and where they're at by their food habits. People who eat food with pleasure and get pleasure from the different stirring of the senses that a well-prepared food experience can bring are my kind of people.

Like Archie says, "Eating is a very personal thing; you can't eat with everybody." Some people got such bad vibrations that to eat with them would give you indigestion. I would rather give such a person money to go to Horn & Hardart than to eat with 'em. God knows, I've had some good times eating with my friends. What times! Times, oh, times! I often get nostalgia for the old days and old friends. Like those New Year's open houses I used to have and everyone I loved would come. Even Millie came from Germany one year. She arrived just in time for the black-eyes and rice. And that year I cooked the peas with beef neck bones instead of swine cause so many brothers and sisters have given up swine. I had ham hocks on the side for the others. You supposed to cook the whole hog head but I couldn't. I saw it hanging in the butcher store on Avenue D and I didn't dig it. I left the swine hanging right where he was.

If you eat black-eyed peas and rice (Hopping John) on New Year's Day, you supposed to have good luck for the coming year. Black people been eating that traditional New Year's Day dinner for years. That's why I'm not having no more open house on New Year's Day. I'm going to try something new. Like Kali says,

> It's a New Kind of Day
> It's a New Kind of Day
> It's the love that make
> a New kind of day

HOPPING JOHN

Cook black-eyed peas.
When they are almost done add rice.
Mix rice and peas together.
Season and—*voila!*—you got it.

And speaking of rice. I was sixteen years old before I knew
that everyone didn't eat rice everyday. Us being geechees,
we had rice everyday. When you said what you were eating
for dinner, you always assumed that rice was there. That was
one of my jobs too. To cook the rice. A source of pride to
me was that I cooked rice like a grown person. I could cook it
till every grain stood by itself. What you do is to rub it together
in the palms of your hands and make sure you get all grains
washed. Then you put it in a pot with cold water.

Use 1 part rice to 2 parts water. Always use cold water. Let
it come to a boil and cover it with a tight cover. Soon as it
comes to a boil you turn it to simmer and you cover with a
tight cover. Let it cook for exactly 13 minutes and then cut it
off. Let it stand for 12 minutes before eating.

HOME

Birth, Hunting and Gator Tails

I'm from the village of Fairfax, Allendale County, South Carolina, so is Jasper Johns. Don't know how many people in the town. I do know I'm kin to most of them. The Ritters and the Myerses and the Smarts are from Luray and Estill. I was born across the branch from where Uncle Bubba lives now. Cousin Amanda was the midwife for me and my brother. We were seven-month twin babies. I was born first and Cousin Amanda didn't know that there was another baby. Cousin Amanda said that he stayed in the womb too long. I was three pounds and my brother was six pounds but he died.

I was so weak they put me in a shoe box and put the box on the wood-stove oven door. That was a kind of incubator. My mother says it was a case of touch and go for a while, cause she got the childbirth fever. She said, "I'm sorry child you'll have to fend for yourself" and started to throw me in the fireplace but all praises due to the gods Aunt Rose caught me. When I go down south now they treat me so good, cause they know that I wasn't but three pounds when I was born.

Everyone always says, "Well do Jesus. To think that you wasn't no bigger than a minute when you was born and now you six feet tall and strong and healthy and you got two fine children of your own. The Lord works in mysterious ways His praises to behold."

I don't remember too much about the house across the branch where Uncle Bubba lives, but I remember a lot about Monk's Corner. We had a big house and a lot of land. That's important! Some land! Black people got to have some land! Haygood and Daddy used to go hunting and bring back all kinds of animals—squirrels, rabbits, possums, coons, anything they could get. Sometimes they used to take me along. I loved it. I've been oiling and shooting guns and rifles since I was very young. When I was a teen-ager I was embarrassed for anyone to know that I knew how to shoot rifles. It seemed a very unhip thing to know then but now I'm glad for the head start. We'd get up early and go deep into the woods. We would take some food and some corn whisky. They gave me a sip or two of the corn likker. My father said if I drank it at home I wouldn't sneak and do it later. He was right. I don't smoke, and drinking hard likker was never no big thing with me. One of my favorite meals after a hunting trip was grits and

SMOTHERED RABBIT

Take a rabbit, cut him up and let him stand in salty water for 30 minutes. Dust him with flour and salt and pepper and brown in a heavy skillet (using ¾ oil and ¼ butter). The pan's got to be very hot. Brown well on all sides. Then cover with a layer of thin-sliced onions. Brown onions in same pan. Then add 1 cup hot water. Cover and cook very slowly for about an hour. If you prefer, you can stick the whole skillet in the oven and bake it very slowly till the meat's tender.

Or

SQUIRREL

Brown the squirrel just like you do the rabbit. Only difference is if you don't want smothered squirrel you leave off the water and you just let the squirrel drain on brown paper.

The winter that I was nine he went hunting and brought back

VENISON

Soak several hours in salt water. Have enough water to cover. Remove and dry. Then rub the poor deer with salt and pepper and butter. Lard him with peanut oil. Put him in a roasting pan and add onions and garlic and carrots. Roast in a hot oven approximately 20 minutes to the pound. Baste the poor deer often with his own juice. The meat of a young buck is more tender than the meat of a doe.

STEWED COON

It's best to use young coons! Cut up into small pieces and soak in salt water for ½ hour. Remove the fat and dry. Season with salt and pepper. Roll in flour and brown and cook until meat falls off the bone.

Then add potatoes, rice, onions, carrots, bell peppers, okra and tomatoes and let cook for 30 minutes more.

GRILLED QUAIL

Clean and wipe and dry your quail. Then salt and pepper it.
Brush with a mixture of melted butter and peanut oil and
place in a shallow pan in a very hot oven and bake until
tender. Brush often with the butter and oil mixture.

CORN MEAL MUSH

Take about 1 quart of boiling water and to approximately 1
cup of corn meal add some salt and cook in a covered double
boiler. If you haven't got a double boiler then cook in a pan
of hot water. Place the pan in a pot of hot water and cook
for 45 minutes about.

Serve the quail and the drippings over the corn meal mush.

PEACOCKS

Are too beautiful to be eaten and I don't think the Creator
meant for people to have peacock feathers sitting in vases
on window sills. If I was Jimi Hendrix I'd get rid of that
vest. It is said that peacock feathers bring bad luck and I
believe it.

PHEASANT

Under glass is supposed to be an epicurean delight. I've never
been able to eat pheasant because it is such a beautiful bird—

all those beautiful iridescent feathers. I feel the same about pheasant as peacock. But if you do cook pheasant here are some tips.

1. Do not pluck too soon after shooting.
2. Although the cock is more beautiful, the hen is better to eat.

KANGAROO TAIL STEW

You know they got it canned and imported here from Australia. Cut the tail of the kangaroo in small pieces. Stew down for 3 hours and when almost tender add onions and turnips and carrots. Strain the grease and serve.

OXTAIL STEW

See kangaroo tail stew.

OXTAIL SOUP

In a BIG soup kettle cook the tail. When done remove meat from bone. Skim the grease and add barley and cook for 30 minutes, then add potatoes and onions and cook for 15 minutes and then add a can of whole tomatoes. Cook for 20 minutes and then add a box of frozen mixed vegetables. Cook for 10 more minutes.

ELEPHANT TAILS

Bracelets made from the tail of the elephant are said to bring good luck but only if someone gives you one. Never buy your own.

BEAR

Indians used to use the grease a lot. You take the paw of a cub and you pack it in clean mud and bake it. Let it cool and remove the clay. The hardened clay will remove the hair as you remove the hardened clay. Then you simmer the paw all day (you have to start before 10 A.M.). When tender serve it like ham.

My cousin Betty Ritter, Uncle Bubba's daughter, gave me a recipe for gator tails.

BETTY'S BARBECUED GATOR TAILS

Parboil the tail and cook in a covered roasting pan with your favorite barbecue sauce.

Note: Gator tails are not to be confused with:
1. gator pears which are avocados.
2. gators which are $125 shoes made of gator skins.

We stayed in Monk's Corner until we came to Philadelphia. We left there soon after the mule stomped me in the head and knocked me out. The nearest hospital was in Orangeburg but they didn't take colored people anyhow. So they took me to the doctor in Brunson. The doctor said that I would live but I'd be retarded. When we got home Daddy shot the mule dead.

The Smarts, the Ritters and Chief KuKu Koukoui

My grandfather Cleveland Smart had a dream. Cousin Hesikay Smart come to him and said your child will be a girl, name her Verta. *Et voila* my aunt Verta. My aunt Verta had a dream when my mother was carrying me, and Cleveland Smart come to her and said, "Name that child of Frank's Verta." Aunt Verta was a beautiful woman. She was delicate boned but had the Smart strength, and she had them Smart eyes, fire brown. We never called her Verta. As a matter of fact it was me who changed the spelling—she spelled it Virter. We called her "Suit," pronounced like *put*. She was good to me. She was tribal.

She would cook for all our cousins who would come through Philly. Even when she hadn't seen them or had never met them. She would say, "They my family. I got to do what I can for them." Like Stella says, "It ain't nothing but some food." I dig digging your people. That is why I go home at least three times a year, and if I can't make it, I make sure the children do. That love of your tribe is important, and if it doesn't happen in childhood, I don't believe you can acquire it.

When you are tribal you don't have slots for loving—you love. You can find a different kind of love for everyone. You love Cousin Blanche cause she was your granddaddy's sister's child; "Aunt" Belle, even though she ain't really your blood aunt, but you feel just like she was kin to you. What I mean is, it (being tribal) gives you a big heart.

Aunt Suit used to cook the best liver and onions. We would have them with grits or rice.

AUNT VIRTER'S
FRIED LIVER AND ONIONS

Have your liver sliced not too thick and not too thin. About ¾ inch is my vibration. Let your skillet get real hot (use bacon grease). Meantime salt and pepper and flour your liver, then brown on each side very fast. Then lower the flame and add thinly sliced onions and a tiny amount of hot water. Cook for a few minutes on each side.

If you cook it too long, it will be watery and tough, so *fait attention!*

* * * *

Chanel was not the first person to mix stripes and polka dots with prints. Estella Smart was the first person I ever saw. Estella Smart is my grandmother and she taught me a lot about sewing and cooking. She was also the first person I

saw in a custom-made (she made it) bathing suit of up-
holstery fabric. Everywhere she goes she creates her own
climate of beauty.

When my grandfather Cleveland Smart died she left South
Carolina and came north to seek a better life. She came to
Philadelphia and kept her family together and managed to
buy a house in the jungle (nickname for North Philadelphia).
I liked the house on Norris Street. Junior and Mary (Aunt
Virter's children) and I had some good times in that house.
When Mother Dear first got the house Aunt Virter and Uncle
Willie and Junior and Mary lived on the third floor and we
lived on the second. We weren't there for a minute before
Mary had punched holes in the wall with a broom handle. My
grandmother had a fit and jammed us all against the wall
to find out how and why and who. Mary said, "It was the
ghost of Mr. Selkowitz." The late Mr. Selkowitz, the former
owner. My grandmother said, "What do you mean?" Mary
went into a long story on how Mr. Selkowitz appeared to
her and she was scared so she got the broom handle, and
everytime she saw his image she would strike out at him—
thus the holes in the wall. My grandmother went for it that
time.

* * * *

Estella Smart is avant-garde. To tell her full story is a book.
Last year she was engaged and I had already bought the fabric
to make her wedding dress to this dude but she broke it off.
I don't think she is ready to give up her freedom.

I was sorry cause I was going to be her matron of honor
and I had never been one before. She was going to elope to
Elkton, Maryland. When she told me that she was thinking
about marriage to Mr. ———, she said, "Although he is not
a geechee he do have salt-water instincts like us."

I remember when we used to go to Atlantic City summers she would swim way out and the lifeguards would blow the whistle. I was embarrassed cause she was my grandmother, and nobody's else's grandmother could even swim let alone cause a commotion by riding the waves in the Atlantic Ocean. She worked in a factory at Twentieth and Callowhill for twenty years. Not one day in that whole time did she carry sandwiches for lunch. She would get up soon in the morning and fix something "boiled." She would put some greens and rice in a jar. And at work she'd put the jar on the radiator to warm. Or she'd make biscuits and fry a piece of chicken. Her favorite piece of chicken was the last piece over the fence.

Every Good Friday we would go to the Four Paws movie house to see *King of Kings*. We would take our water and pillows. Mother Dear (that's what we called her) didn't think it was healthy to drink behind other people. The pillows were to sit on. She didn't believe in sitting directly behind somebody else, either. When we visited people she would turn the sofa seats over or spread a piece of cloth to sit on. Sometimes now I find myself doing that. When I was at the Sorbonne and I was selling books at the pouvoir noir stall in the courtyard during Occupation '68, I had to go to the bathroom real bad but I was scared cause there was a rumor that there was a VD epidemic plus at home we never went to bathrooms in public places but if we couldn't help it and if we just HAD to we would take some lye soap along to wash ourselves afterwards. Since the French mail was still *en grève* Mother Dear couldn't send me any . . .

LYE SOAP

Empty a whole can of lye in a big iron pot and put in 1½ quarts of water. Stir with a stick until the lye is dissolved and then let it cool down. Then you take all your tallow that you have been saving on the stove in cans for months and you melt it. Being very careful that it don't get much hotter than body temperature.

Mix your lye and tallow solutions together and stir till it is uniform and thick. Then put it into a box lined with wax paper and let it stand in a warm room for four nights and three days. Cut into cakes. It is good for everything. We wash our hair and bathe and do laundry with it. It is very economical because you just have to buy the lye. The tallow you can save each time you fry something. Coffee cans make good containers for tallow savers.

MRS. ESTELLA SMART'S BRAINS

Under cold water remove the veins and membranes. Rinse the brains very quickly. Then put in a saucepan and parboil with salt and pepper and a little vinegar and a little garlic. Let cool and when the brains are cool cut them up, roll in flour and brown in oil. Then add beaten eggs and scramble all together.

MRS. ESTELLA SMART'S
LIVER AND LIGHTS STEW

Parboil the lights. Cut up the liver in chunks. Cook lights for 20 minutes. Let cool and then cut up. Put cut up liver and lights in pot with enough water to cover and then add chopped up onions and red pepper and salt. Cook and when almost done add potatoes and carrots. When done adjust seasoning and serve.

MRS. ESTELLA SMART'S
MOUNTAIN OYSTERS

Cut mountain oysters in half and parboil for 10 minutes. Then
season to taste. If they are too thick then dip in Aunt Jemima
pancake flour. Fry in fat.

*   *   *   *

I remember when Uncle Howard came up to visit. We were
mad because we didn't want to "sit" with him everyday. But
Mother Dear made us. We told him that everything was
electric—the stairs, the floors, the chairs. Being from Estill
and never having lived with electricity he believed us. Our
purpose was to keep him immobile. He was. He was scared
to death of all the "electric things" and each day when my
grandmother got home she would find him sitting in a chair
humming and smoking his pipe. Uncle Howard told her that
he thought he was going to cut his visit short because the
electric was too much for him. My grandmother asked him
what he meant and when she found out we had tricked him
we were in trouble. We had cut out all Uncle Howard's
phone calls too because we said the phone was electric and
he wouldn't bother to call or even talk when people called
for him.

After the house was "de-electricized" Uncle Howard wasn't
afraid to talk on the phone and he started calling his friends.
At this time Uncle Howard was in his late seventies. One of
his friends was a lady from South Carolina that we called Aunt
Sally. Aunt Sally was in her seventies too. Aunt Sally would
come over to visit and we had to cook for her and Uncle

Howard. One day Mary said let's put Black Drought in the stew, and milk of magnesia in the rice. So we did and it was awful. Poor Aunt Sally. She kept saying, "This beef stew is different" and Mary said that she had cooked it with a spice that Uncle Zander brought back from cross the pond. When my grandmother found out what we had done this time we were really in trouble. Thank God, Aunt Sally wasn't seriously sick. She just had a case of diarrhea for several days. Uncle Howard didn't eat any of the stew because he was still eating some of the smoked ham he had brought from home.

* * * *

My Grandmama Sula was very beautiful. She was a Myers before she married Granddaddy Ritter. The Myerses got a lot of Indian blood and it sure showed on Grandmama Sula. She had high cheekbones and long black hair. Mostly I remember her sitting on the porch of the house that Granddaddy built when they first got married, smoking her pipe and rocking in her favorite chair. That was a wonderful house. Probably looked like a shack to a lot of people but I loved it. It was so full of love. Now Uncle Bubba lives in another house that some white folks gave him. He put the house five hundred yards from the old one. It is a much better house but it's not the same. Granddaddy built that house by his self and Grandmama planted the flowers in the yard. We have fig trees, peach trees and pine trees in the yard. On Saturday mornings we would get switches from the woods to make brooms to sweep yards. You tied all the switches together and used them to make brooms to "sweep yards" every Saturday morning before we went to town. I was lazy and used to claim that I was having another attack. I had a rare disease that you only get from being born weighing three pounds and you can't work too hard. At least that was my version. My cousins' version was LAZY.

When we were in the cotton fields I would get "sunstroke" and have to rest. While everyone else was way up in the field picking a row an hour I would steal a little bit of cotton from each bundle. I would put it on mine and when time came to weigh each sack Uncle Bubba would say, "No wonder the poor child is worn out, she can pick as much cotton as a grown person." But they soon discovered my secret and left me back at the house with Grandmama Sula to help her cook for the midday meal. I had to shell so many field peas that I would have rather been back in the field, almost. I loved Grandmama Sula cause she was so softhearted and kind to us. She let us do things that she never let her children do or at least that's what Mama says. She could cook and she would sometimes cook Indian food for us. Mostly I remember the hoe cakes she made.

In Paris I used to eat what they called crepes—a thin pancake. They are very good but I don't make them. In Paris on the Rue Grégoire des Tours there is a place that serves nothing but crepes and jelly—honey—and anything you can name. About twenty different crepes 'n' things. The only beverage they serve is cider. Crepes are delicate to make and you have to have an expensive and fancy pan to make them. I prefer hoe cake of bread like Grandmama Sula used to make.

GRANDMAMA SULA'S HOE CAKE

2 handfuls sifted corn meal
pinch salt
pinch soda and melted bacon grease
    (if you eat swine—peanut oil if you don't)
about 1 cup sweet milk

Mix all together and wait a few minutes to see if more water is needed—then pour the whole mixture into a hot greased heavy black cast-iron skillet. Put it on your plate. Pour some thick syrup and sop it up and it's out of sight. Hoe cakes are also good with pot likker. Hoe cake got its name from the hoe. Slaves would cook batter on the flat edge of the hoe in the fields for the noonday meal. You don't have to cook it on the metal part of the hoe cause we ain't slaves no mo'.

As for pancakes—go and use Aunt Jemima and they always come out right. The best syrup is the kind you can't get up here—that sticky stiff sweet stuff that is homemade. I found some stuff called "Georgia Syrup" in a supermarket in Allendale and it's the nearest thing to homemade that I have ever tasted. Ann Jones puts it over her black-eyed peas. It's that good. Of course, she's from Georgia, and Georgia colored folks are crazy as Geechees. Look at William White and Marion Brown! I never had any success trying to make pancake batter from scratch. Raymond St. Jacques made breakfast for Billie Smith and me a few years ago and he made the most delicious pancakes. Raymond used to live at Twenty-ninth and Park Avenue South on the top floor of the house that used to belong to the "Girl on the Red Velvet Swing." The house is gone and there is a parking lot there now but every time I go by I think of those wonderful . . .

PANCAKES SMITH ST. JACQUES

Beat 2 eggs and then add (alternate dry and liquid) pinch salt, ¾ cup flour, 2 tablespoons sugar, 1 cup milk and 1 teaspoon cinnamon. For the last thing add 4 tablespoons butter (melted). Drop from spoon in a skillet greased with peanut oil and turn when you see a thousand holes. Cook on both sides and serve with Georgia syrup or whatever kind you like.

Note: Pancakes taste better when the batter is made an hour or so before cooking.

*   *   *   *

You won't find any heavy baking recipes in this book cause I'm not a good baker. I have never lived in a place that had a decent oven. Those oven temps from the 5 & 10 cent store don't work and for most baking the temperature is very important. I use cake mixes and doctor them up. That way if they don't work out I don't feel as bad as when I start from scratch. For the poundcake that I use you need a pound of everything. But it is not complicated—even my oven couldn't mess it up. This poundcake got me a proposal of marriage.

I knew a fine fly young man who used to spend the times we were together telling me about his girl friends. I was like his sister. Being a shy person I searched for a way to let him know that I was interested in an incestuous relationship. I invited him to dinner at my home but he arrived at 6 P.M. instead of 7 P.M. and I was scrubbing the floor, frying chicken, cutting collards and making

POUNDCAKE

Cream together 1 pound sugar and 1 pound butter and add 1 pound flour. Then add one at a time 12 eggs and a pinch of salt. Beat it all together by electric mixer or 900 strokes by hand. Then add 1 tablespoon vanilla extract, 1 teaspoon lemon extract and 1 teaspoon mace (the spice not the gas)

and mix together for a minute to blend the flavor, then put in a loaf pan lined with greased wax paper. And bake in a slow over for 1 hour.

The fine young man loved the cake. He said that he had a thing for girls who get on their hands and knees to scrub floors (I never use a mop) and who can cook. The dude asked me to marry him but I didn't.

*   *   *   *

Rose Ritter Polite was my aunt who saved me from the fireplace. She was fine as she could be. Chandra acts just like her. My mother always tells how Aunt Rose used to scream and holler when she had to get her hair combed. This one Sunday morning Grandmama Sula was combing it for church and she started going through her act. Falling out, calling on the Lord and all; so Grandmama sent my mother across the swamp to borrow the scissors from cousin Sas P. Ritter. They cut it all off, then got in the horse and buggy and went to Sunday school where everyone laughed at Aunt Rose who promptly cussed them out there and then. My mother says she was very embarrassed. Sounds just like when Kali talks about how Chandra acts up. Aunt Rose used to cook

COW PEAS

Remove all the peas that look weird and wash and soak in cold water. Cook in some kind of boiled meat until done. Cow peas by the way, came here via the slave trade, from Africa where they grow wild. Dried cow peas are called black-eyed peas.

She could also make the best

RED RICE

Fry smoke bacon in skillet and then add your fresh tomatoes. Cook for a hot minute. Add cold cooked rice and cook for another 20 minutes.

I really loved Aunt Rose. I didn't see her much as I should. But whenever I did it was always pleasant and warm and she always had a pot on the stove. She lived in a furnished room in Harlem on 131st Street.

She paid $100 a month for being in a dump. The bathroom was on the next floor. It was shared with four other people. Her "kitchen" was a former closet. The whole apartment was in reality the "parlor" of the converted brownstone. Cooking those good meals there would be way beyond the capacity of most women. Isn't it amazing that black people in spite of all the misery and oppression have been able to keep on keeping on? Len Chandler has a song called "Keep on Keeping on." The fact that we survived middle passage is a credit to our race. Black people still have a lower suicide rate than whites. White folks just seem not to be able to take it when times are hard. Look during the depression how they jumped out windows when they lost their money. If they had known about neck bones and dry peas they might have realized that they could survive.

A Roman named Marcus Apicius is said to have been one of the the first Italian cookbook writers. He was the male Perle Mesta of the early Roman empire. But he lost his stocks or inflation hit, anyhow he blew his fortune and he killed himself rather than live without *la dolce vita*.

One thing about being poor—you can only go up. Those

Romans were something else. A typical banquet might start at 5 P.M. and go on until 5 A.M. When a guest arrived at the banquet the host provided the guest with something comfortable, a muslin garment that allowed a lot of freedom to eat the endless courses. Sometimes they changed garments between courses. Might have been because they ate with their hands and they was more likely wiping their hands on the garments. Between courses slaves would wash their hands for them with perfumed water. The host sometimes provided them with silver toothpicks and some folks even had an enema between courses. A typical banquet menu might be pickled vegetables, venison, hare, peacocks' brains and larks' tongues, chestnuts and raisins soaked in honey. They didn't have sugar then—they sweetened everything with honey. Dried figs were very popular. Goose cooked with chestnuts, wild boar stuffed with ten and twenty blackbirds. A slave would cut the boar's belly and the birds would fly out. Another slave would return them to the kitchen and they would be cooked and served in another course. Sometimes a slave runner would be dispatched to fetch a fresh mullet. Asparagus was a popular Roman vegetable. They believed it would prevent heart trouble. Turnips, cabbage, apples, radishes, cucumbers and collard greens were also standard Roman fare. It is said that the Romans took collards to France and England. By the way, the Romans had a welfare problem too! Many a senate debate was around the issue of how to tighten up on the welfare chiselers.

When Aunt Rose died I couldn't go down for her funeral (she died in New York City but we all gets buried in Miller Swamp or Calvary) but the children went with my mother and Deacon Wilson. My mother said that the Ritters from all over came down. She said there were so many people in the church that they had to make an announcement that the side aisles were family too. Usually the middle aisle is for the family and side for distant cousins and friends.

After the service they went back to Uncle Bubba's house
and everyone came over to eat. The family all brought pans of
food so that Aunt Hattie didn't have to cook. Aunt George
Ann brought a big pan of

POSSUM AND TATERS

Try to get hold of a young one. They are the most tender.
If your possum isn't young, parboil him. Rub the cleaned
and dressed possum with salt, black pepper and red pepper
seeds and sprinkle with flour inside and out. Add water and
cook in a covered roasting pan in the hot oven for 1 hour. Then
place sweet potato halves in pan around the possum. Adjust
water and add more if needed. Cook covered for ½ hour,
then remove cover. Sprinkle possum and taters with brown
sugar, lemon juice and melted butter and bake uncovered
until beautiful brown.

* * * *

BURNING DRAFT CARDS AIN'T NOTHING! My great
grandfather burned his "free pass" for love. He was straight
from Africa and he was proud and tall. He bought his freedom
from his master. A lot of people like to say they are the
descendants of African chiefs. I have been through that stage.
Did I tell you all about that? We put out a magazine and it
was cheaper to do it in England—so we went to Dover.
While we were there, it was so dull that we wanted to do
something to liven the place up so we said that I was Princess
Verta from Tabanguila, an island near Madagascar. The following article appeared in the *Kent Express,* Dover, England,
January 30, 1958.

PRINCESS VERTA STUDIES OUR WAY OF LIFE

Latest in the long list of royal visitors to Dover is an African princess who is here to study European customs.

Charming Princess Verta, 21 years old, comes from the tiny island of Tabanguila, between Madagascar and the African mainland.

Her father, Chief Kuku Koukoui, rules over his tiny kingdom unhampered by European administrators, although the island is regarded as a French possession.

The Princess is staying as the guest of Mr. R. Sheridan, a plastics manufacturer, in his luxury seafront flat at The Gateway.

Princess Verta speaks fluent French but no English, and wears exotic and colourful flowing robes. She has just completed a two-year study course in Paris and is visiting this country before returning to her tiny island.

NEXT RULER

The only child of Chief Kuku, she is being groomed as ruler of the miniature kingdom, the first woman to be chief of Tabanguila.

Princess Verta hopes to take back to Tabanguila a number of souvenirs of her visit to this country, and these will include a piece of the famous White Cliffs of Dover.

"I never imagined them to be so white," said Princess Verta through an interpreter. "I heard of them, of course, before coming to Europe but never envisaged anything so magnificent."

Princess Verta has visited the castle and the historic Maison Dieu Hall but finds more interest in the harbour and re-development which is taking place.

"I find the future more exciting than the past," she said. "Tradition has its place, but new buildings and homes are important."

She said that her own tiny community lived a simple life and that she would not try to impose any modern ideas upon her return.

"France and England have changed my outlook, but I know what my own people want from life," the princess said.

Anyway my great grandfather wasn't really no chief, but he was a man. He was a Jack of all trades. He could make anything. I remember Granddaddy Charlie weaving baskets and making wagons. He told us how his grandfather from Africa had taught him. My great great granddaddy had an African name. I don't know what it really was, but folks say it was something like "Ifana." Anyhow, this is what happened:

He bought his freedom, but fell in love with a very beautiful slave girl named Namomma. Since he did some work for the master of Namomma, he saw her often. He was free; she was a slave, and slaves couldn't get married like other people—not really. They didn't know what to do. He wanted to have her for his wife, so he asked the master how much it would cost for her freedom. The master said $500. The master thought that was a fair price cause she would make a good breeder.

For seven years my great great grandfather worked to get that $500—and when he got it, he went to the master and offered to buy her freedom. The master said that the price had gone up to $1500. My great grandfather knew it wouldn't be possible to save that much money, so he took out his free man's pass and burned it, and offered himself to the master as his slave as long as Namomma was his slave. He made one clause in the bargain. If the master ever tried to sell her or any of their children, he said to kill him first. Otherwise he would kill the master and his whole family. And he said if the master tried to sell them after he was dead, he and the ghosts of his ancestors would put a curse on the house of Johnson and all their children thereafter would be cursed with ugliness. Master Johnson was so taken back that he let his daughter go and gave them *both* free issue passes.

* * * *

I had an uncle named Costen. They say that education run him fool. They say that he knew more than anybody in the Allendale County including white folks. When he died he was 112 years old, they say. I remember he used to walk from Allendale home every day and that at least ten miles, and he was at least ninety-seven then.

He could recite poems and add up as many numbers as you could throw at him. All in his head, too. He didn't need to write nothing down. Uncle Costen used to tell us stories about slavery. How it was and how it wasn't. One story that he told was about the Underground Railroad. He said that sometimes they would be in the middle of their dinner when the stops (homes that hid slaves en route to freedom) got word that a slave or slaves were coming through that night. They might even have some neighbors or even members of the family there who were not cool. Everybody wasn't in it all together like the Browns (John & sons) so they had to have signals to let each other know that tonight it would happen. Uncle Costen said they had a special dish they would serve called

HARRIET TUBMAN RAGOUT

Brown stew beef in peanut oil and add water and let come to a boil. Simmer for 2 hours. Then add potatoes, carrots, onions and turnips. Cook till vegetables are just about done, then add okra and cook for 15 more minutes.

This is a true story so relate it to your family and smile and say, "Guest who's coming to dinner?"

My grandfather's uncle, Willis Ritter (Uncle Costen's brother), was famous. He was famous in Sycamore, South Carolina. He taught Latin and math. He was born a slave and lived until he was ninety-eight. He once told my mother the story of how his father ran a "bootleg pass ring."

When the slaves heard that the "Yankees is coming" they decided to go meet them half way. If they were stopped and didn't have a pass they would just say "I belongs to the next plantation, I's on de road home." Road to freedom was more like it.

Thousands of slaves left this way. Uncle Willis' father could read and write so he made up free issue passes and had what they called a "bootleg pass ring." He sold the passes for sacks of flour, sacks of corn, bacon, hogs, etc., and *comme ça* he managed to feed his family.

On Emancipation Day he remembers hearing . . . Thank Gawd Almighty . . . Free at last . . . Great Gawd Almighty free at last.

*　*　*　*

Every summer we would go home for the Fourth of July. That was Uncle Bubba's birthday and every year we would have sort of a family reunion. Uncle Bubba and Uncle Simmie would butcher a hog and we would have barbecue *for days*. Aunt Hattie would make a dozen pies and two dozen cakes. Oh, what good times! Uncle Bubba would buy a special No. 2 tub to fill up with lemonade. If we missed the Fourth, then for sure we would go for the big meeting at Miller Swamp every third Sunday in August.

As a matter of fact, today is the third Sunday in August and I'm in fun city. But the big meeting this year won't be too much fun because Aunt Julia died. They would have buried her today, but due to the big meeting they will bury her tomorrow. I wonder if Cousin Jaspher and Cousin Liza brought dinner this year. They always have some good dinners. Aunt Julia was their mother, so I doubt if they did.

At the big meeting it seems to be that everyone brings dinner and just exchanges plates. Everybody is insulted too if you don't take one of their plates. I would take them all and try to eat it all too. They would bring the food in pans. I tell you it is a feast. Pans of potato salad, collard greens, rice and chicken. My favorite was Cousin Gussie's

COCONUT CUSTARD PIE

Beat 4 eggs until well beaten; then add ½ cup sugar, salt, 3 cups scalded milk, 2 teaspoons vanilla and a ½ cup grated coconut and pour into an unbaked pie shell. Set the Pyrex dish in hot water and bake in a moderate oven for 45 minutes.

* * * *

When we go south by train, I always get excited around Denmark cause after Denmark is Ulmers and after Ulmers is Sycamore and after Sycamore is Fairfax. From Sycamore I can see Uncle Bill's house and between Sycamore and Fairfax I pass the house I was born in. It's falling apart but in my mind's eye I can see it as it used to be. Right near to it is where my mother and father got married. The house burned down but the trees are still there. Uncle Bubba always tells of how pretty Mama looked standing under that tree in her white dress. After Uncle Bubba meets us in Fairfax we pass the same road by car and I always lean out and yell and act crazy. On the same road we pass Uncle Costen's house and I always yell out to Serge and Miss Belle. They always wave back and shake their heads and say, "That fool doll is home again."

After we pass there I get quiet cause it is a swamp and there are big tall Spanish moss trees and I'm scared of the way they look. Also Modestine and Bozie and Sister and Juanita left me in that swamp once. I never got over that. They left me cause they said I was acting too citified. I was complaining about how far we had to walk to get from Miss Nuit's house to Uncle Bubba's. I said in Philadelphia we got trolley cars. So they ran ahead and left me in that swamp. When I came out I was mad and didn't talk to them for two days. I played by myself.

Modestine and Bozie are my mother's sister Luella's children. John and Jerry, Betty and Helen and Juanita and Brenda are Uncle Bubba's children. Glen and Debbie, Barb and Brother are Uncle Bill's children. Sinah and Sister are Uncle Simmie's. Fester is Aunt Rose's son. They are my first cousins on the Ritter side. We grew up together and have had some wonderful times. I just never forgave them for leaving me in that swamp. Everybody except Sister and Juanita got some children. One of my happiest times is when their children and my children get together and I watch them grow together.

Every time someone from home comes up or we come back we bring food. Uncle Bubba used to send us boxes of home-made sausages and "puddin'." Cousins Mon Ritter and his wife Princess made the best puddin' I have ever had. Last time I was in Fairfax we had too much stuff in our luggage so I decided to put the extra clothes in a cardboard box but at the railroad station the white stationmaster said, "No good. We don't accept boxes any more." I asked why and he said,

"Because too many of you all too many times done put sausages and ham and stuff in them boxes and they gits up north and the stuff rots in the boxes before you all picks them up." So I had to buy another suitcase.

Philadelphia, Mrs. Greenstein
and Terrapins

Our house on Erdman Street in Philadelphia had a coal stove in each room except for the kerosene heater in the living room which we rarely used. Erdman Street was on a dead end. We paid seventeen dollars a month and used to be behind in the rent (most of the time). We had two rooms on each floor, three stories. The third floor was all mine. I used to play school and give plays. I was actor, director and audience all in one. In the winter we all slept in the bedroom on the second floor cause we didn't have enough money to make fires in all the stoves. My mother used to get a basket of wood and a bag of coal from Mr. Daniels. They was twenty-five cents apiece and mostly we got credit and would pay him when the eagle flew on Saturday. We had two stoves in our kitchen—one gas, one wood. When they cut off our gas we could still take care of business on the wood stove. Sometimes Mama would cook on the wood stove anyhow. She said it seem like the food just taste better on it.

During those days, I was one of those "key" children. I wore the house key around my neck. After school I'd let myself in and I wasn't supposed to let nobody in. Nobody. If God came I was supposed to say that "my mother is not home and I'm not allowed to have any company." God never came by but some kids would try to get me to come out. Sometimes I'd sneak out and old Mr. Simmons would always tell my mother who would tell my father who would knock the hell out of me. I did not like Mr. Simmons.

Miss Tinnie, Mr. Simmons' daughter, was the only one on the block who had a telephone and she let us get calls there but we had to pay her ten cents when we received a call. Being an only child and being alone in the house gave me lots of time to experiment with cooking. Since nobody could come in and I couldn't come out I had lots of time. I used the time to raise hell. I got into a lot of things and lots of trouble. Once I gave a dance concert in the back yard. We had a portable gramophone and a few race records. Most of the records were gospel. I danced to them. Sure enough Mr. Simmons told my mother that I was committing blasphemy dancing to church music.

Another time I set the house on fire. It was my birthday but it was a Thursday and we didn't have any money. My mother said to wait until Saturday but I just couldn't. I wanted it when it was. I had no faith. Because the same thing had happened at Christmas. They told me that Santa would come on the Saturday after Christmas but the rent was due on that Saturday and he didn't come at all. So I had lost the faith and I wanted my party then.

Mama brought me some pink-coated cupcakes and she went back to work for Mrs. Krader on Ridge Avenue. I was supposed to go back to school at 12:45. Took me five minutes to find some birthday candles for the cupcakes and have a party of one. I put the candles in the window and started singing "Happy Birthday" to me. As I was singing a gentle spring breeze was blowing and the shade danced over the candles and caught on fire. In a minute the shade was blazing. I started spitting on the fire but nothing happened, so I ran to get a bucket of water. I couldn't find the bucket. Then I remembered that Mama had loaned it to Mrs. Wilson so I ran downstairs to get a big pot but all the pots were soaking in the sink. My mother would be so tired when she came home from cleaning up Mrs. Krader's house all day that she didn't feel like scrubbing pots and she didn't trust me to clean them well enough. If she found a speck of grease on a glass or a dish she scalded it three more times. We had no hot water and had to heat water for dishes and baths. Yet Mother washed the dishes twice and scalded them three times.

Anyhow I ran back downstairs to get the icebox pan under the icebox—it was always full cause I'd forget to empty it—and ran to throw it on the fire but by this time the whole window frame was on fire and rapidly spreading across the wall. Good old Mr. Simmons had already called the fire department and I heard them coming up the street. I decided that there wasn't nothing I could do for the fire so I dropped the basin, shut the bedroom door and ran up to the third floor and got under the bed. The firemen put out the fire. It was the first time they had been on our street in four years and all the neighbors were there. One of them ran to Ridge Avenue to tell my mother that the house was on fire and her daughter was missing.

Mama almost had a heart attack cause that was always her biggest fear while I was alone. Mama came running. Meantime I'm still under the bed. I heard the firemen ask, "Where is the bad little boy that did it?" The neighbors said, "It weren't no bad boy, it was that child." The firemen said, "Well if we find that child she will go to jail." I was trembling and worried cause I was late getting back to school. My teacher was real mean. Old lady Eaton would make you stay after school for thirty minutes if you were late coming from lunch and my father would raise hell if I was late coming from school. I was uptight. Just then my mother arrived and came directly to the third floor to look for me. She hugged and kissed me and asked me to explain what happened. I was a real bright reader and I had read that a doctor said that children had traumas. I thought a trauma was something that could happen to make you speechless and hysterical. So I tried that. I stuttered and stammered and got hysterical and cried and said that I couldn't remember because I had a traumatic experience. My mother gave me two minutes to recover my memory or else receive an emotional experience on my behind. She had never read that book. I recovered in thirty seconds.

After that all the neighbors used to ask me when I was going to have another birthday party, and to be sure and invite them. They said, "This time that child has taken the rag off the bush." Oddly enough that was my only fire. It is odd too, cause I used to cook all the time. Poor Mother never complained about all the food I messed up.

* * * *

I would use up all the food experimenting and she would never fuss.

I now realize how uptight it must have put her cause we were so poor and every bit of food counted. My mother is a remarkable woman.

The family she worked for on Ridge Avenue had a hat store. They lived in back and on the two floors above. Mama made eleven dollars a week and at Easter Mrs. Krader would sell us hats, pocketbooks, gloves and stockings on credit. The hats were always at least ten ninety-five and the dark stockings (red fox, etc.) cost more than the beige. Mama would pay a dollar or two each week until it was paid off. Sometimes it would take damn near till the next Easter. Whenever they got some new furniture they would sell us the old. That's how we got our gas stove, etc.

Mama would sometimes take me to work with her. On those special occasions like Passover, Zelda's wedding, etc. Mama used to also help serve (for overtime) when they had big dinner parties. Those occasions were my first introduction to gefilte fish, lox and bagels, challah, halva, Mrs. Grass's chicken soup, cottage cheese, kasha and noodle and raisin pudding.

It was at one of these parties my mother met Mrs. Greenstein (her future employer), a lady from North Carolina. Years later when I went back to check out Ridge Avenue I had to laugh when I saw the hat store. For years I thought the Kraders were rich and lived in a mansion. The reality was that they were hardly even upper lower class. I don't like hat stores to this day.

Mrs. Greenstein (of late my mother's former employer) now lives in Miami and during one of her visits to Philadelphia visited my mother. Hearing of the cookbook she sent this recipe via my mother to me.

SPONGECAKE

1 box Duncan Hines Yellow Cake Mix
1 3-ounce box lemon-flavor Jell-O
⅔ cup milk
⅔ cup Wesson oil
4 eggs

Combine all ingredients except eggs. Beat eggs and add to other ingredients and mix. Bake in preheated oven, 325 degrees, for 50 minutes.

My best friend on Erdman Street was Shirley Daniels. We had a good time growing up together. We used to get in more trouble than even my daughters Kali and Chandra do now. We were that far out.

Miss Lessie (Shirley's mother) could really make good . . .

BANANA PUDDING

Make a custard with about 1 pint sweet milk, yolk of 3 eggs and ½ cup sugar. Add vanilla and pinch of salt. Slice 5 bananas and place alternately in a baking dish with about 2 dozen vanilla wafers and the custard. Meringue the whites of the eggs, add a bit of sugar and place on top of the banana mess. Bake in moderate oven for 12 minutes.

* * * *

My daddy belonged to the 20th-Century Motorcycle Club. I remember *Harley-Davidson. Chrome. Shiny Chrome. Real Fox Tails Hanging from Each Handle Bar. Leather Jackets with Shiny Studs.*

One time he had one with a sidecar. That was the one I liked the best. Nobody else on our street had one and no other eight-year-old could go flying through the air like me. I loved to ride fast. I would scream, "Faster! Faster!" and my father would laugh and say we are already doing 250. Are you trying to get to outer space? I guess I was cause now I go there with Sun Ra and his Solar Myth Science Orkestra.

Some Sundays the whole 20th-Century Motorcycle Club would go over to New Jersey to Lawnside to party. Everything was closed on Sundays in Pennsylvania because of the blue laws. They could cook some barbecue in Lawnside. Lord give me strength, it was out of this world. This is the closest I could come to it

LAWNSIDE BARBECUE SAUCE

Mix together well and cook:
1 bulb garlic, diced
1 cup sugar
3 whole lemons (use juice and rind)
2 cups chopped onions
1 bottle tomato catsup
1 bottle Louisiana Hot Sauce
little bit dry mustard
some vinegar
some water
some butter

Mix and cook until it looks like it wants to come to a boil, but don't let it. Use on ribs—pork or beef. That's up to you.

Once Daddy had an accident on his motorcycle and broke his collarbone and his right arm and his left leg. When he left the hospital with his casts he decided that since he would be laid up for a while he should spend the time in a place with good vibrations. So he got on his motorcycle and went to Fairfax. Years later we drove south for a visit and as we were getting gas in a filling station in one of those real cracker towns I began to feel nervous—the man was looking at my father very strangely and I was worried. *The Smarts are famous for their long legs and short tempers.* My father noticed the strange vibrations the man was throwing out at him and said, "Wonder if that bukra is ready to come up missing cause that's what's going to happen if he don't stop looking at me." Finally the man walked up to my father and said, "Are you the nigger who pass through here in '47 with his right arm in a cast and his left leg in a cast and his neck in a brace?" My father said, "Yeah, I'm the nigger and Frank Smart's my name." The man said, "I thought it was you. I ain't never forgot your face. Mr. Smart, let me shake your hand cause you a bad nigger."

My father and his brother Alexander used to have a battle of food. That is, one time Uncle Zander would cook something and then next time my father would try to top it. And next time Uncle Alexander would . . . you dig. The result was that we had some tasty dishes. Uncle Zander is a merchant seaman and now a head cook on the high seas. Of all the many dishes he has cooked, and all the spices he has used from the seven seas, I still like his corn muffins the best.

UNCLE ZANDER'S CORN MUFFINS

        3 tablespoons flour
        3 tablespoons corn meal
        1 teaspoon baking powder
        ¾ cup milk
        1 tablespoon some kind of short'nin'
        pinch sugar

Beat all and put in muffin tin or skillet and cook until brown.

FRANK SMART'S
COLD HOT SMOKED TONGUE

Soak tongue at least 12 hours in cold water. Cook in a Dutch oven on simmer. Remember, start from cold water and bring to a boil slowly. After it has cooked for 1 hour add carrots, red crushed pepper, bay leaf and whole peppercorns. Simmer until tender or about 2½ to 3 hours. Let tongue cool and remove the skin, then chill and slice it.

*   *   *   *

Frank Smart was slick. His image as a great fisherman lasted until the day he died. I asked him how come he always caught more fish than anybody all the time and how come he always won the bet (sometimes as high as twenty-five dollars) that he would catch the most? He said, "Simple. What I don't catch I buy from other fishermen!!!!"

I love fish. You know the expression, "The blacker the berry, the sweeter the juice." Well the fishier the fish, the better I like it. Straight up fishy. There was a fish store on Ridge Avenue in Philadelphia called Porgy and Bass. My mother used to get catfish from there and make

CATFISH STEW

Wash the catfish and cook in a Dutch oven with onions, salt and pepper for about 45 minutes in enough water to cover.

FISH HEAD STEW

Is delicious. My mother used to get the heads from the fish market on Ridge Avenue for five cents a pound. She would stew them down with onions and bell pepper. Served over grits, head stew is an epicurean delight. I had other fish stews and my mother's head stew is the best. When we were coming home from Denmark on Icelandic Airlines, we stopped in Iceland. The whole trip was weird and unreal. On the plane at ten in the evening having a steak dinner in the midnight sun (it was that time of year) listening to Aretha Franklin on the earphones. Then we stopped in Iceland for three hours where we were served fish stew. I thought what the hell am I doing in Iceland eating this terrible fish stew. Another time was when I tried to make a bouillabaisse. I spent a lot of money and it didn't turn out very well. I later found a food shop that sells bouillabaisse in the can for 89¢. It's not bad, at least not as bad as mine. I've had *zuppa di pesce* in Rome and it just didn't make it. Ain't nothing like the real thing.

ROE

We used to have roe all the time, not shad. The so-called gore-mays dote on shad roe but it is expensive and the shad fish is too bony for me. Mullet roe is delicious with grits. Do not overcook. Cook in butter or oil in a covered skillet for 15 minutes. No seasoning except salt and pepper needed.

SARDINES

I LOVE THEM. We used to have sardines in mustard sauce or tomato sauce over grits. The plain sardines are good over grits or in a sandwich with a slice of onion. I do not eat Portuguese sardines because of Angola.

SALMON

Poor as we were we never ate nothing but sockeye salmon. I still don't. One of my favorite breakfasts is grits and salmon.

In a skillet fry some bacon and when almost done, add chopped onions and cook for 5 minutes, then add a can of sockeye salmon.

OYSTERS

Are in season in the months of the year with the letter "r" in them. They have a nutritive value and can be eaten many different ways. I like them directly from the shell with lemon juice. I dislike oyster stuffings. They are very good rolled in a batter made of cracker crumbs and eggs and then fried in butter. I have to pull your coat to one thing. Don't look for a pearl in oysters. True pearl oysters are not edible.

Whenever Daddy went crabbing it was a real treat. We would have enough crabs for all of Erdman Street. Wasn't but seven families on the street and five of them from South Carolina. We would boil the crabs down in a No. 2 tub and eat for days, adding a quart of beer to the water—sometimes.

Other times we'd fix

CRAB SALAD

A little bell pepper, a little celery, fresh mayonnaise and chopped onions. Mix with the crab meat and add cayenne to your taste.

CRAB CAKES

Combine crab meat, bread crumbs, salt and pepper, chopped onions, a little flour and just enough heavy cream to hold it together. Brown in peanut oil.

Note: Be sure you always remove the dead man from the hard-shell crab. The dead man is the spongy part under the shell.

SOFT-SHELL CRAB

Clean and dip in flour (or egg batter) and fry in butter. You may eat all the soft-shell crab.

TERRAPINS

Ain't nothing but swamp turtles. They used to be plentiful on the eastern seaboard. So plentiful that plantation owners gave them to their slaves. Now they are the rare discovery of so-called gore-mays. White folks always discovering something . . . after we give it up. By the time they got to the bugaloo, we were doing the "tighten up." By the time they got to pigs' feet, black people were giving up swine. By the time we get to Phoenix. . . .

First Cousins and the Numbers

My first cousin Queen Esther is married to a maharashi or mahara or anyhow she married a rich Indian (the kind of Indian Chris was looking for before he discovered Ray Charles—I mean America). They live in Madras and have lots of servants. She and I exchange letters all the time. She told me that even though they have all those servants she still does her own cooking. Queen Esther comes from out by Beaufort way and the Geechees round there will work roots on you in a minute. So I think that she is scared that someone will fix her with roots while they are fixing the food. Queen Esther wrote that she makes curried black-eyed peas. She says that black-eyed peas are prehistoric and that they don't really know who the motherland of black-eyes is—Africa or India. She says that they got mustard greens there too and has promised to send me some Indian spices soon as I send her a couple of boxes of hominy grits.

* * * *

Another one of my first cousins hit the numbers and took off to the West Indies to live. She writes me about once a month and sends recipes. She goes from one island to the other like she was going from Brooklyn to Queens.

For the past few months she has been in Jamaica. She wrote me an' she was very excited because she thinks that the maroons in Jamaica are the same maroons who were here. That is, she says that they came from the same part of Africa. During slavery, in South Carolina and Georgia there were many maroon camps. The maroons were the slaves who ran away to the swamps and set up camp. Sometimes they built cabins and sometimes they had forts. It was impossible to break up the camps. Some camps lasted for years. The maroons in Jamaica took to the hills and haven't come down yet.

It is a possibility that it's the same tribe in the south now. Some people say Gullahs, some say Geechees and some refer to us as maroons.

In the last letter I got from her she sent me a bunch of information about a bunch of different kinds of yams and a delicious recipe for coconut sweet sweet potatoes.

Dear Verta Mae,

Did you know there are all kinds of yams? These are only a few. There are many many different types here.

WHITE YAM hill people in Jamaica dry for hard times.
SWEET YAM is the sweetest.
RENTA similar to white yam but sweeter.
YAMPY very delicate and hard to cultivate. It's a very dry and refined yam.
YELLOW dry and powdery.

Then there is a yam called nigger yam. I won't even deal with that because after all a yam is a yam is a yam.

Your cousin,

Markana

COCONUT SWEET POTATOES

Parboil sweet potatoes and let cool, then slice and cook in skillet in butter and a little bit of peanut oil for 20 minutes and then add coconut cream and brown sugar and cook until done.

* * * *

Rose Sullivan is the mother of my neighbor Yvonne and she is a dynamite cook. I want to thank her, too, for giving me some of the following West Indian recipes

RASTIFARI MEAT PATTIES

½ cup olive oil
2 medium-size onions
6 cloves garlic
1 pound chopped chuck steak
½ pound chopped pork or Italian hot sausage
1 large can peeled tomatoes
1 small can tomato sauce
1 small can tomato paste
1 teaspoon salt or to taste
2 teaspoons red peppers or cayenne pepper
4 bay leaves
2 teaspoons orégano
1 teaspoon sugar

Heat oil in heavy skillet, chop onions and garlic and brown in oil. Mix chopped beef and pork together, sauté in oil, stir with fork until meat separates and is slightly browned. Add tomatoes and tomato sauce and paste to beef mixture, add salt and pepper, bay leaves, orégano, sugar to beef mixture and simmer slowly for 3 hours. Cool and store in refrigerator for 24 hours.

PIECRUST FOR MEAT PATTIES

6 boxes piecrust mix—water
2 cups flour

Mix piecrust mix with water, following directions on box. Roll piecrust mix out on floured board ɛry thin. Cut 4-inch circles of crust and stack one on top of the other, making sure they are well floured. Place 1 teaspoon chilled meat mixture in each piecrust circle, fold in half and press edges together with fork. Place on floured cooky sheet and bake until crust is brown, about 20 minutes, in 400-degree oven. Serve hot. Yields about 6 dozen.

SOUSE—FROM VIRGIN ISLANDS

pig's head
pig's feet
salt
parsley
thyme
hot pepper
black pepper
onions

Clean the swine's head and feet thoroughly. Cover with water and boil until tender. Then put into clean boiling water, add salt, etc. Cook for 1½ hours. Remove souse from stock. Remove the larger bones. Make a sauce from strained (run through a sieve) stock with limes and hot pepper. Garnish with parsley and sliced limes.

Serve at room temperature. Sauce is made up of approximately 3 cups stock, juice of 3 limes, plenty of hot pepper.

MARKANA'S FRIED PLANTAINS

Cut plantains in lengthwise slices, then cut each slice in half— if you want to.

Fry in an iron skillet in peanut oil until golden brown. Drain on brown paper.

ESCAVIACH FISH JAMAICA STYLE

5 pounds fresh fish (sea bass, butterfish, porgies or kingfish)
juice of 4 lemons
1 tablespoon onion salt
1 teaspoon seasoning salt
1 teaspoon black pepper
paprika
3 cups corn oil
1 cup cider vinegar
½ cup water
1 tablespoon sugar
1 teaspoon salt
2 large onions, sliced
2 teaspoons Tabasco sauce
  or 2 teaspoons ground dried red pepper or to taste
1 tablespoon whole allspice

Have fish cleaned. If they are large, cut them crosswise in 2-inch slices, leaving heads on. Clean thoroughly. Season with lemon juice, onion salt, seasoning salt, black pepper, paprika. Let stand 3 to 4 hours. Pat fish dry with paper towels. Heat oil in heavy skillet very hot and fry until brown. Turn over on opposite side and brown until crisp. Remove from oil onto paper towels to remove all excess oil. In skillet that has had oil removed and been cleaned, put vinegar, water, sugar and salt and bring to a boil. Add onions, Tabasco or hot pepper to taste and whole allspice. Simmer 5 minutes. Place fried fish in casserole, add layer of onion mixture and layer of fish. Let stand overnight. Serve hot or cold. Serves 12.

CODFISH AND ACKEE JAMAICA STYLE

2 pounds salted dried codfish with bones
2 pounds salted dried codfish without bones
2 large onions
2 large green peppers
4 cloves garlic
1 can tomato sauce
1½ cups oil (coconut, olive or corn)
hot peppers to taste
2 cans ackee

Cut onions in half and slice. Cut green peppers into ½-inch chunks. Chop garlic. Brown onions and garlic in oil slightly, add tomato sauce, hot peppers and simmer 5 minutes, then add green peppers and cook 5 minutes more.

Soak codfish in about 4 qts of water overnight. Pour off water and add 4 more quarts water. Bring to a boil and let cook for 5 minutes. Let stand in water until cool to remove most of salt from fish. Remove bones from fish and separate boneless fish into flakes and mix both together. Add to sautéed mixture, simmer in heavy skillet for 10 minutes. Strain ackee in colander and fold into fish lightly so they will not fall apart. Serve with kidney beans and rice. Serves 12.

JAMAICAN CURRIED GOAT

Take goat meat and cut in cubes. Then wash it; then salt and pepper it. Let stand for 1 hour. Work the salt into each piece of meat with the hands. Add curry powder, crushed red peppers, scallions and onions and work all ingredients into the meat. Let stand for another hour.

ATTENTION: Goat must be cooked in a cast-iron pot.

Place pot on stove, cover and cook. Do not add water. The meat gives off a great deal of liquid. Stir constantly to bring the bottom meat up to the top. Cook for 2 hours or more or until the meat is very tender.

TURTLE STEW
from Virgin Islands

1 stewing turtle
1 large onion
2 tomatoes
sweet pepper
3 medium potatoes
1 cup sherry
salt

black pepper
garlic
capers
Worcestershire sauce

Scald turtle. Remove hard shell. Clean well. Then season with
salt, black pepper, garlic. Sprinkle with capers and Worcestershire sauce. Let stand for 1 or 2 hours. Chop onion, tomatoes
and sweet pepper and sauté in oil and butter. Add turtle and
allow to brown. Then add 2 cups of hot water and steam
until tender. Add potatoes. Simmer for ½ hour. Add sherry
just before serving. Serve piping hot.

SALT FISH CAKES

½ pound salt fish
onions
hot pepper
1½ cups tomatoes
½ cup flour
1 egg
parsley

Soak fish in water until soft. Squeeze water from fish and
grind meat in meat grinder. Sauté onions, pepper, tomatoes and
parsley. Add to fish. Make balls and dip in flour and egg. Drop
by spoonfuls into fat. Fry a golden brown.

AWAY FROM HOME

'59

Being tall and digging the theater was what made me go off
to Paris in '58. I always dug theater. When I was three years
old I won a prize at the children's day contest at Miller Swamp
for reciting an original poem. In grade and junior high school
I was still in programs. But I never joined the dramatic club.
I was too shy and too insecure about my looks. I was tall and
skinny. I mean skinny—not thin but skinny. Kids teased me
all the time and it was terrible. I slouched my shoulders and
never stood up straight. I got skipped a few grades and was
always the youngest in my classes but I was always in the
back of the line because I was the tallest.

High school was the worst. I wasn't allowed to have dates
and even if I had been I don't think I would have had a very
good time. I was convinced that because I was so tall my fate
in life was to be an old maid. People were always saying that
the girl has to be shorter than the boy and all the boys that I
knew were shorter than me. The high school prom was a drag.
A friend of mine suggested that I ask Wilt Chamberlain cause
he lived on the same street as her aunt. But he was out of

town. I went with a nice young man named Sonny but still I was miserable. I really believed that everyone was laughing at me because I was two inches taller than Sonny. I knew that I was destined never to marry. What man would want a six-foot-tall woman? Not tall from the waist up but from the waist down. What man would possibly want a woman with long legs? I thought I was a freak and the bohemian life was the only one for me because they were tolerant of everyone.

I went to a lecture by Raymond Duncan (Isadora's brother). After the lecture I talked to him and he convinced me that the bohemian life was the only one. So I decided to go to the one city where the bohemians lived and let live and off I went to Paris. The boat ride itself was a trip. I was scared to death but excited as hell. I was nineteen and off to see the whole world. Dig that. My mother and my aunt Virter came to Hoboken to see me off on the *Ryndam* February 7, 1958.

I had no idea of what was in store for me but I made a vow to meet it. I didn't get seasick even though it was my first boat ride. I was so full of digging everything and everyone. I talked to everyone and tried to give an image of being a very sophisticated lady. I said I was an actress going to Europe to do some film work. Most people could guess that I wasn't but it didn't matter to me. I rented me a deck chair and I spent a lot of time watching the ocean. When we arrived at Rotterdam in Holland and I was on the pier claiming my baggage, etc., I looked around and then it hit me. I was a long way from home. I checked out the people speaking another language, looking different and I had a few bad moments. I wished I was home again but remembered my vow and so off I went to my hotel. The first day in Europe I slept. I hadn't slept too much on the boat because I just could not rest on the water. So back on land I slept half the day. The next day I decided to explore the town. I walked around and looked at Rotterdam. After a few minutes I got nervous.

Everyone was checking me out. I just wasn't used to people looking at me. They wasn't used to black people I guess. I don't know what the reasons were but I knew I felt weird when the trolley car stopped and everyone was grinning and waving at me. The only reason I went to Rotterdam was it was the most northern point and I wanted to see all I could. It don't cost but a few extra dollars to debark at Rotterdam instead of Le Havre. So there I was. I was a little scared but I had made up my mind that I was out to see the world. I stayed in Rotterdam two days and then I got the train down to Paris.

Paris has got the best public relations firm in the business working for them. Man, when I arrived there I could hardly believe it was really me. To think I was in Paris, France. I found a small hotel on the Left Bank, of course. That's where all those people (bohemian) that I was looking for were. I did meet a lot of people. In the beginning I was very shy about talking to people in cafés but later I adapted to that Paris habit and I'd start conversations on my own. I enrolled at the Alliance Française. There I met a six-foot-tall Swedish girl named Charlotte and we became roommates. We shared the room on Rue de Fleurus. As a matter of fact down the street from Gertrude Stein's house. We weren't supposed to but we cooked in our hotel. Charlotte introduced me to the high art of cooking on an alcohol burner. She would cook three-course meals on it; it didn't take me long to catch on and we gave the best dinner parties in the hotel. Course I couldn't fry chicken or cook no chitlins but we did manage to eat a bit better than the food that was served in the student place.

I met a lot of people, Arronne, Helene, Anita McCullen, Countess Vespinami, Bernard, Bob Strawbridge Grosvenor, Jonathan Kozol, Herb Kohl, Lucien and Claire Fleury, Dickie Dell, Alex Campbell, Malik, Bernard Boston, Gerard. Some of them became close friends. One of them I married. Arronne is still my friend and I stayed at her house when I went back to Paris after almost ten years.

Helene is still on the Avenue Duquesne in the beautiful house, and she rented the bottom floor to the girls and me when we went there. When I was there I saw Anita. I had dinner with her and Bernard. It was a Monday and most stores were closed but we had a delicious dinner. Since the meat stores are closed on Mondays Anita had to make do with one pork chop and two lamb (baby) chops. But the meat wasn't missed. First we had a salade de tomates, then the chops and a delicious

CAULIFLOWER A L'ANITA

First parboil the cauliflower. Let cool and separate the flowerets. Make a white sauce with butter, flour and milk. Then add Romano and Parmesan and Gruyère (or Swiss cheese). Put cauliflower in casserole alternating with the sauce. Cover with bread crumbs and bake.

Anita then served a green salad and bread and goat cheese. We had wine and liqueurs after dinner and it was really one of the best meals I ever had in Paris. I hear that Alex Campbell has become a famous folk singer in England. I remember he used to sing all over the Paris streets. He is Scottish and it was the first time I ever heard someone sing "You Take the High Road and I'll Take the Low Road" with feeling.

Jonathan Kozol has written a book on the school system *Death at an Early Age*. Herb Kohl wrote another book on schools called *36 Children*. Lucien Fleury is a famous painter and this past year I saw Bernard Boston again too. I also saw the Countess Vespinami in Milano. I had dinner with her and her daughter Marvy. The dinner was delicious. We had a huge antipasto and then

PASTA

Take your desired shape pasta and cook according to directions. Make a sauce of salt, pepper, cream, grated Parmesan cheese and lots of butter.

After the pasta we had veal Milanese, then salad and cheeses and fruit and coffee. The only sour note was that Marvy told me that she was getting married and going to South Africa to live.

French people can be so narrow-minded. I got so sick of hearing "Oh, madame, *en France* we do it different." "Madame, perhaps where you come from, but *en France.* . . ." I got to the point where after I would ask for something and they got that weird *en France* look, I would say "yeah-yeah" I know—*en France.*

One Thanksgiving in France a bunch of us expatriots decided to have a Thanksgiving dinner. I ran around to find an exotic food store that sold America canned goods and finally found one near the Madeline where I bought cranberry sauce and Maxwell House coffee.

We were living on Git-le-Coeur, and since we were the only ones who had a kitchen we cooked everything there.

Dickie Dell made

AMBROSIA

Cut and pare fresh pineapples. Pare oranges and remove membrane and separate in sections. Slice bananas and sprinkle sugar over the fruits and sprinkle juice of fresh lemon and add freshly grated coconut. Let stand in the icebox for several hours.

And we made the potato salad and fried chicken together. We got some pumpkin and were going to make a pie but couldn't find anyone with an oven. When I bought the pumpkin it looked so strange that I figured if I ask the woman how to cook it I can tell from her answer if it is pumpkin or not. So I asked and she said, *"En France nous faison le potage."* I thought to myself—"Damn, this can't be no pumpkin if these people make soup out of it. So I asked her again and I said, "You mean you make a tart?" *"Non, madame jamais! En France nous faison le potage."* I didn't believe her. I was sure that she was crazy but it was true *en France* they make . . .

PUMPKIN SOUP

Sauté 2 diced onions in 4 tablespoons butter in a saucepan. After onions are golden brown sprinkle with flour and cook for 1 minute. Then add 2 cups puréed pumpkin, 4 cups chicken broth, a pinch sugar, salt and pepper and bring to a boil. Cook covered on simmer for ½ hour. Remove from saucepan and put through mill and return to saucepan to heat through. Add ½ pint of light cream and serve.

When we lived on Rue Git-le-Coeur in '59 we had a two-eyed gas burner and we ate most of our meals in.

The shopping was a gas on the Rue de Seine. Vegetables looked so wonderful. They were real! Not like those weird-looking ones I was used to seeing in the Acme Market in Philadelphia.

The Rue de Seine was a everyday happening for me. Nobody had a icebox so you had to shop two times a day. In the beginning I only bought familiar things because I couldn't speak French. I would only buy potatoes, tomatoes, etc.

But as my French got together, I got adventurous and tried out the "native food." That was also the first time I heard the expression fagots—I thought to myself these people are too much. Going around cooking fagots—I thought only Africans were supposed to be cannibals but it turned out that fagots were not something you ate but a bunch of wood tied together.

Back home I was used to shopping in the Acme Markets so it was an experience to go to a different store for everything. It shocked me coming from Pennsylvania, where you bought wine in the State Store, to be able to buy milk and wine in the same store and see children returning wine bottles like they were milk bottles. Plus in Pennsylvania you got to be twenty-one to be able to purchase alcohol and I was only nineteen so I felt like I was putting something over on somebody.

I was always looking all over Paris for unusual food stores. Henri told me there was a store in Paris that sold frozen lion's tails and elephant tails with green peas. I looked all over for it. Henri was the one who told us about the restaurant, "belly of the revolution," for the students during the occupation May 1968. We never found that either. Marc and I went to dinner at Henri's house and had the best wine I ever tasted (outside of Pouilly Fumé); it was called Pissy-Dur!! Julia translated it into English and said it meant a forceful piss! We listened to Archie Shepp "Live in San Francisco," talked about Julia's father Richard Wright's play *Daddy Goodness* (at that time in New York City at the Negro Ensemble Company) and drank three bottles of Pissy-Dur. Then we went downstairs to a little Spanish restaurant and I had a very good

CODFISH WITH GREEN SAUCE

Fry codfish steaks until golden brown, then cover with a sauce made of olive oil, lots of garlic, some melted butter, juice of fresh lemons, salt, pepper and plenty of fresh parsley.

I remember the first time that I heard John Coltrane records. I was in Paris in '59 and we got a record by Trane called "My Favorite Things." We used to play that record all day and I mean all the day. He would paint and I would read or fool around or cook. One thing I liked to make was . . .

SALADE NIÇOISE

Salade Niçoise is a French name but just like with anything else when soul folks get it they take it out into another thing.

Vigorously stir together in a bowl 6 cold cooked and diced potatoes and ¼ pound cold cooked green beans and 1 chopped red onion and 2 firm medium-sized tomatoes and ½ green pepper and 3 hard-cooked eggs cut in slices and 2 cups of cold cooked rice and 1 can of tuna and 1 can of flat anchovies and marinate for 3 hours.

Then add a mixture of oil and drop of vinegar and lemon juice and salt and pepper and blend the whole thing together and let stand for another hour. Then serve topped with a bunch of salad greens if you want to.

'68

After I'd seen Paris again after nine years I wondered how I could have wanted to live and die in that city. Physically it's beautiful in spite of the coldness of the French people. But, man, when I arrived and saw those black cats sweeping the streets I knew that the third world has got to happen. I know most of the warmest people in Paris. William Melvin, Karen and Kelly and Jessica and Brother Elkton. Tom Harris and Carlene Polite and Marc and Arronne and Gilles, Clair and Fleury and Trevor and Patrick and Jerry and Henri and Julia and Helene and Frank and Jimmy and Marion Brown. Marion came to Noisy Le Sec and I made kalalou for him and Arronne and Gilles and Bugi.

KALALOU NOISY LE SEC

1½ pounds salt meat—
    pigtail
    fat back
    ham bone
1½ pounds fresh fish
2 crabs
3 pounds spinach (kalalou greens)
1 large onion
garlic
12 okra
hot pepper
parsley
thyme
1 tablespoon vinegar
coconut

Boil salt pork until tender in 3 quarts water. Boil fish, remove bones and add to stock. Add crabs. Put in spinach, onion, garlic, okra and other ingredients. Add to stock and boil rapidly for about 30 minutes.

I decided to look up all the people I had known nine years ago in Paris and when I went to visit Helene it turned out to be a good thing. The bottom floor of her house was for rent and so we rented it for a while. It was cold and damp and we didn't have hot water but it was big and beautiful. We loved it plus I had a kitchen and I loved to cook all of our meals in. I immediately set out to find the new markets, etc. Helene lived in what was her ex-husband's father's house. He was a painter and the house was two stories with the first floor a former gallery (where we lived) and the top a huge sixty-foot studio—but all around Helene's house on Avenue Duquesne were modern French high-rise apartment buildings and the section was expensive. So we took the bus over to the Rue de Seine because food was cheaper. I'd cook French-type breakfasts—that is, hot chocolate and bread and jam or marmalade. Our big meal would be at midday. The children adjusted very easily.

After we left Helene's house we found a place on Rue des Ursulines. Our tiny apartment was very hip. It was in a town house that belonged to an old poor Russian countess who charged us four dollars extra per month for the light in the hall. We really had a rotten deal there. The only good thing was that we had a kitchen and a small balcony. I took the apartment because I found it on April 4 (my birthday) and it was on the Rue des Ursulines (Chandra's middle name is Ursule) and we found a hanger in the closet that said Grosvenor House. I thought that was too much for me so I took it. The kitchen was very tiny but I bammed a bunch of nails in the wall and unpacked my trunkful of kitchen stuff and set in to try my hand at

STEWED JERUSALEM ARTICHOKES

Peel and quarter the artichokes and sauté in a skillet with onions and garlic and salt and pepper and butter. Remove to a saucepan and cook with beef broth until tender.

Note: Jerusalem artichokes are not difficult to find. They are swarthy in color and resemble potatoes in shape.

We always had a lot of company on Rue des Ursulines. Teddy used to come and baby sit for me. In return I would cook for him. But Teddy said that he was getting the short end. So it didn't last long. One of his favorites was a dish of meat and chicken that I called . . .

UPTIGHT RAGOUT

Take leftover meat and a couple of chicken legs and add fresh vegetables and rice and cook together until done.

Kali used to go shopping each day for us and she did a beautiful job. One day I sent her for a *demi-baguette* and she came back with a half loaf of *pain de campagne* and two *pain au chocolat.* She said they didn't have any more baguettes and so she got what she could with the money she had.

Up until that time she hadn't let on she could say more than "bon jour" and "merci" in French. Next day I saw the woman from the bakery who told me how beautiful my daughter was and how sorry she was to hear that we were leaving for Russia. I said, "What are you talking about?" She told me that Kali talked to her for five minutes and told her all our business and even said we were leaving for Russia for six months. I asked her if she spoke English—she said that the whole conversation was in French.

We always had lots of company on Rue des Ursulines. One day Pat and Ted and Dave came and all the stores were closed. We only had a couple of thin slices of ham and a few potatoes and eggs in the house so I made something that I called

OMELETTE DES URSULINES

In an 8-inch iron skillet sauté onions and green peppers in butter for 5 minutes. Remove from skillet, then beat 6 eggs in a bowl. In the skillet make a layer of eggs, then onions and peppers, then layer of cooked potatoes (approximately 2 medium-size), then a layer of eggs again, then a layer of onions and peppers, then rest of the eggs, then top with ham slices and cook on moderate flame until eggs are cooked. Cover tightly (about 20 minutes).

Slice like pie. Remove from pan with pancake turner.

And other

EGGS

CAVIAR Overpriced fish eggs that rich white folks serve on crackers.

GOOSE Bigger than chicken eggs but very oily.

DUCK Very good. We use to get them at the poultry market on Ridge Avenue. They too are oily eggs.

OSTRICH Excellent if you can get them. Great to have on hand in case people drop in. One egg will feed six people.

TURTLE These eggs can be eaten raw or cooked.

TERRAPIN See turtle.

There is nothing better than a breakfast of grits 'n' eggs. René makes a dish with bacon and shrimp, onions and bell pepper and scrambled eggs. For scrambled eggs I use a few drops of water instead of milk.

*   *   *   *

Europeans can really be unnatural. Like one thing that used to gas me is in European restaurants people ate fruit with a knife and fork. It didn't take me long to adapt. You know people got to dig that "nigger dialect" is really beautiful. The slaves were just adapting to a language that wasn't their own. They were from many tribes, and plus the masters didn't talk too tough themselves. So they took the English language and did what they could with it and it was beautiful. Black people are the only people in this country who speak English and make it sound musical. Anyhow, back to adaptivity, being the granddaughter of a slave who adapted to the unnatural ways of his master, I, too, soon caught on and there I was eating fruit with a fork. How unnatural can you get! Big juicy orange and you got to take it in forkfuls instead of letting all that juice run on your hands and then licking your fingers. But at the time I thought it was hip. For years I thought it was. Then one day I was back in South Carolina and I picked some figs and stuck them directly in my mouth. I didn't dare tell anyone that I had been eating prosciutto and figs rolled together with a fork.

Same thing with watermelon. I was used to busting melons and sticking my full face smack jam up in the heart of the melon. Here was folks using knifes and forks to eat watermelon. I would never order watermelon in a restaurant, not cause I was shamed, but I just couldn't bring myself to use a knife and fork to eat melon.

WATERMELON RIND PRESERVES

Peel the rind and get rid of the green and get rid of the red. Now soak the rind in lime water for 1 evening and 1 full day.

On the next morning remove rind from the lime water and put in fresh water and soak for 2 hours and then soak rind in salt water for 2 hours. Rinse rinds and cook in fresh water on simmer for 40 minutes. Now add more water. You got to keep adding hot water if the rind turns white. It will turn to nothing but straight up sugar if you don't have just the right amount of water. O.K., now you add sugar to the rind (about 1 pound of sugar to 1 small melon). Boil until clear. Put up in Mason jars.

ATTENTION: WATERMELON AND LIKKER WILL KILL YOU. That's what some people say. Beaver Harris and Donald Hubbard act like they believe it. Every time I see Beaver he starts mentioning a party that I had last summer and we had watermelon and likker. Just because several jazz musicians were here he claims that I was trying to kill jazz.

Donald mentioned the same thing to me at the "soul food party" at Carlos' house in Rome. We had watermelon and champagne and Donald was a little nervous about it but I told him that they probably meant American melons and corn likker. I told him I was sure there was nothing to worry about because the champagne was French and the watermelons were Italian.

* * * *

We went to visit Millie in Germany since we were already in Europe. The train ride there was miserable! People keep looking and falling into fits of laughter. I didn't speak German but I knew that Negra was universal. Also I recognized *schwarze* which means dark which meant us. Anyhow the worst part was the conductor who helped me get a *couchette* (sleeping berth). He had been very kind and even got off the train in Cologne with me so that I could change money so I could pay for our *couchette*. I said thank you so much and we settled down for the night. But just as I was about to drop off in comes my "conductor friend." At first he said he was checking to see if we were all right. Then he started panting heavy and hard. "Please give me a little kiss. Just one kiss. I know Negroes have good kisses." I said if you don't get out of here I will cut you and you know Negroes have knives. So he left. I locked the door. But I didn't sleep good. He was the conductor and had the master keys. He didn't come back but it spoiled my train ride.

When we finally got to Millie's village she wasn't home. But everyone knew who we wanted to see and they let us in. We stayed a few days and the girls had a good time playing in the village. Kali said the only thing that annoyed her was that everyone took so many pictures. I told her, they would say it was for posterity. Twenty-five years from now "Remember when the schwartzas passed through" and have pictures to prove it.

MADNESS

Forty Acres and a Jeep

I get mad real fast. Madness is everywhere—all around us. I get mad when people mess with my children—taxis don't stop and people call me out of my name. I dislike plastic flowers, instant coffee, gossip, subways, hospitals, working from nine to five, people who point their finger in your face, Con Ed, opera, elevators, bank tellers, the jet set, dogs with jeweled collars, Cadillacs and I can't stand people with shiny cars and dingy children.

In this two-child, three-car society, people take better care of their cars than they do their children. Filling themselves up with all them pills. (A little boy told me that Jack and Jill went up the hill to smoke reefer and pop pills.) Talking about they can't feed all the people here. Why? Why not? This is the richest country in the world. Any citizen should be given at birth the guarantee of a life free from hunger. And tell *me*, what is a second-class citizen? You either a citizen or you're not. And that reminds me about my forty acres and a mule. I'll take the forty acres and a Jeep.

Annie Ruth who is on the welfare says that it isn't necessary for black people to feel uptight because they are on the welfare. She says it ain't nothing but retroactive pay from slavery. Probably the interest from their forty acres. White folks act like they gonna die cause the price of food is steadily rising. They would starve for sure if they had a welfare budget to eat off. And it is true that the supermarkets raise the prices on the days that the checks arrive. And the slop that they sell to the poor black neighborhoods is a sin on their souls. Huntington Hartford should really pray to his God for forgiveness. Instead of building that ugly museum in fun city he should have cleaned up those nasty supermarkets in the ghetto. I heard that they bring the rotten stuff from Park Avenue down to Avenue D and up to Harlem. Really the smell in that supermarket on Avenue D is worse than Kitty Litter. I stopped going in there after I found more roaches in there than I had at home. These New York roaches are working together with the people who make the spray. You buy a spray and they disappear. You tell your neighbor that you used such and such a brand and she uses it and they go away. In the meantime, they come back to your place and you try something else and they leave again and go to your neighbor and you tell her to try the other brand and it goes on and on and the old roaches always return.

And don't even talk about the mice. We got a few that just come out any time they please and smile at you. Chandra can talk to them and the other day she told me that the mice told her that they didn't like grits and to stop leaving the grits pots on the stove to soak.

One day, a friend of mine who is a revolutionary was visiting and a mouse was in the bathroom. I screamed, "Kill him, kill him" and he said, "Hell no, not me." He said call the fire department. I said that if he didn't kill the mouse and flush him down the toilet I would tell everyone that he was going to kill white folks but was afraid of mice. It took thirty minutes to convince him, but he did. Just goes to show you everybody talking revolution ain't making it.

He had come over for dinner that day and we had . . .

CHICKEN STEW WITH DUMPLINGS

Take a fowl and wash and clean him and salt and pepper him and put him in a pot and let him cook with a bay leaf or two and some small onions and a bit of butter. When he is just about done, in a bowl, mix ½ cup flour and 1 egg and ½ cup sweet milk and salt and 1 tablespoon of shortening. Mix it all well together and drop by the spoonful into the pot with the fowl. Cover with a tight cover and cook for another 30 minutes.

Corn meal dumplings are also delicious.

Name-calling

A lot of new foods were brought to this country via the slave trade like watermelons. They were cultivated thousands of years ago in the Nile Valley. When David Livingston got to Central Africa he found watermelons growing wild and sweet. Egyptians make salted roasted watermelon seed. The Russians make a beer.

Some other things brought via the slave trade were sesame seeds (sometimes called benne seeds), yams, cow peas (black-eyed peas), peanuts and

SO-CALLED OKRA

Boil your meat and then add washed and carefully trimmed so-called okra. Do not cut the tip. Cook for 20 minutes.

If you are wondering how come I say so-called okra it is because the African name of okra is gombo. Just like so-called Negroes. We are Africans. Negroes only started when they got here. I am a black woman. I am tired of people calling me out of my name. Okra must be sick of that mess too. So from now on call it like it is. Okra will be referred to in this book as gombo. Corn will be called maize and Negroes will be referred to as black people.

A SO-CALLED OKRA GUMBO

Fry some bacon in an iron skillet and save the grease. Add chopped onions, tomatoes and so-called okra and salt and pepper and water. Cook for 1 hour, then add a can of maize and cook for 20 minutes. Add the grease you saved and adjust the seasoning and serve on rice.

FRIED GOMBOS

Wash and dry the gombos and sprinkle with corn meal, salt and pepper and fry in peanut oil. You may need to sprinkle salt again after they are fried.

GREEN MAIZE MUSH

Use green maize on the cob. Scrape the cobs and mix the green maize with milk, salt, coconut water, sugar, powdered cloves and vanilla extract. Cook on simmer until it thickens, stirring often with wooden spoon.

People are always calling *people* out of their name, too. Calling the Germans—"krauts." Calling the Italians— "guineas." They call the English—"limeys" and the French

FROGS

Take a frog and cut off his back legs and throw the rest of him to the dogs. Soak the legs in ice water for 8 hours. Keep adding ice to keep water cold. This will make the legs swell and grow whiter. Then remove and dry and salt and pepper and coat with bread crumbs. Fry in butter until golden brown on both sides. Serve with butter browned in same pan and lemons.

ROAST GUINEA

Clean guinea hen, stuff with your favorite dressing and rub with fresh lemon and spread guinea with soft butter. Bake in a hot oven for about 1 hour. Baste often with butter and lemon juice mixture. Did you know that guinea fowls are from Africa?

The so-called Irish potato is not Irish at all. As a matter of fact it didn't even reach Ireland until somewhere around 1570. It got the name Irish potato cause it was the thing that brought the Irish through the famine. Potatoes are native to South America. Its name is really *patata*.

IRISH POTATO SOUP

In a saucepan sauté onions and white part of green onions for 3 minutes. Then add peeled and sliced Irish potatoes. Add salt and pepper and chicken broth. Cook until potatoes are soft. Soft—like you were going to make mashed potatoes. Then put the soup through a sieve several times. Put soup broth in saucepan and add cream or half and half.

I don't like to call people out of their name, but a friend of mine gave me a recipe for

CRACKER STEW

Take a can of any kind of soup and add 1 box of any kind of frozen vegetables and then add 1 cup of Minute Rice. Heat and serve with toasted crackers on top.

My "Cracker Stew" friend gave me this recipe too—for a bread called

DYNAMITE BLACK

Mix together 1 cup sugar, 1 cup dates, 1 cup walnut meats, 2 tablespoons flour and 1½ teaspoons baking powder in a bowl. Then add 3 beaten eggs and some vanilla extract. Bake for 35 minutes in a moderate oven.

I got another friend who is down on Chris Columbus. She says he was really out to lunch because he went looking for spices (didn't grow none where he came from) and went the wrong way. Then when he got here claimed that he discovered the people who were here. Worst of all he called them out of their name. They taught him how to make

SO-CALLED "INDIAN" PUDDING

Scald and pour 1 quart of milk into a saucepan with ¾ cup yellow corn meal. Let them cook together for 25 minutes. If you have a double boiler use it, cooking the milk and meal on top. If you don't have a double boiler do the best you can. Mix in a bowl—salt, cinnamon, ginger, molasses and butter and 3 eggs (well beaten). Mix up the meal mixture and the ingredients in the bowl and then pour the whole thing into a well-greased baking pan. Place the pan in another pan of hot water and bake for 1 hour.

You can serve it plain or with ice cream.

When old Chris got here the Indians were eating rockahominie and sukquttash, the Indian names for hominy grits and

SUCCOTASH

Use fresh-off-the-cob maize and fresh butter beans and salt. Cook until almost tender, adding black pepper and butter.

Askutasquash is a Massachusetts Indian name and it is from that name that we got the word

SQUASH

Take gourd squash and halve it and scoop out the pulp. Sprinkle brown sugar, nutmeg, butter or bacon grease and a couple of sausages (small beef or pork) and bake (wrapped in tin foil).

This recipe is for spiced Brazil nuts and don't let no smart aleck call it out of its name and say spiced niggertoes. You just be correct and say

SPICED BRAZIL NUTS

Melt 1 stick of butter in a big black skillet. Add shelled Brazil nuts. When they start to brown sprinkle well with powdered ginger. Stir often. When they stop browning remove from heat and sprinkle with kosher salt.

Hospitals Ain't No Play Pretty

I don't like hospitals and being in one ain't no play pretty. I had to have my appendix taken out. Thought I would die, but thank you Jesus, I'm living to tell it.

I was in the Beth Israel Hospital and that was an experience. First off the doctor said he thought it was appendicitis. But when the nurse came and handed me the paper to sign, it said exploratory. Although she had already prepped me I got up to go. Oh no! I said. Exploratory means that you can operate anywhere on me you want to. I ain't no fool. You want my heart. You all took poor Clive's heart but you won't get mine. I know you need black hearts but this is one that you won't get. You can go get your mother's and the doctor can get his mother's but you won't get mine.

The nurse got the doctor who said, "Hello young lady, I hear you have a problem." Yeah I said you're damn right I got a problem—you all trying to cut out my heart. He said in a weird voice, "Don't be silly. Whatever gave you that idea?" And I went off again. He saw that I was nutting out so he told me that I was right. He said you should not sign anything that you don't believe in. Don't sign. Go home and if it isn't appendicitis you'll probably die and if it is it will rupture and you'll die, but go on go home. I signed.

I woke up in more pain that I can ever remember and my mother was there and Oscar and Dorothy and Ayischia, all the way from Washington, and Sandra and Howard who got lost looking for somebody else. They ran into Dorothy who guided them to my room.

In my room everyone spoke Yiddish except me. Everyone ate kosher food. There were four of us. To tell the truth wasn't no black folks on that floor except me. A nurse's aid told me that I was in there only because I was an emergency and that the next day I would be transferred to the old building. That evening my roommates had company and everyone was talking in Yiddish. I felt really weird and I knew it was a case of move on over or we'll move on over you. I checked the whole thing out and knew what I had to do. I called Ella to go to my house and get my wraps and my geles and my lapas and my Che Guevara poster and my framed photo of Rap Brown and my Stokely Carmichael *Black Power* book and bring them to me at once. She did.

I put a ring on every finger, at least nine bangles on every arm, Ella's purple wrap, and wrapped my shoulders in Kenti cloth. Read my "Episodes of the Revolutionary War" by Che and sipped fresh orange juice that my mother sent. I never transferred!

The doctors came to see me very often. I was getting tired of them because there were so many interns coming to check me out. The surgeon had experimented on me.

All these hospitals experiment on black folks first. They had used a wire instead of stitches and when they removed the wire it was a hairline scar called a "bikini cut." They hadn't done it to many people so I had lots of interns coming to check me out. About the fourth day when the doctor came

I asked him how long did I have to stay. He said you can leave any time. Soon as someone comes to pick you up you can go. He said, "By the way"—looking at Che's book— "when the revolution comes don't forget that I saved your life and that I did a beautiful operation on you." It was really weird.

I did get the feeling that they wanted me to leave. While I was there they talked about me like a dog and talked about my friends. When people came through the main door downstairs the man would say, "Grosvenor," and give them my room number. I even got permission for Kali and Chandra to visit me. I called them on the phone and Chandra said where is my mama? I said I'm here. She said no you're not Verta cause if you were we would have been able to see you in the hospital. I said, "No children are allowed." She said Verta would have found a way. You are an agent. What have you done to my mother? She started to cry saying that the outer space agents had taken her mother. I got on the phone and went to the head nurse who said no good. No children ever. I said well can I go down to the lobby in a wheel chair. She said no good either. I said please I've got to convince my children that I am me and no agents entered my body. She looked hard for a moment and said no!

So I went into my act. I said, lady I am not legally or morally bound to your laws and I'm going down. She said you'll be in trouble. I said my children are having a trauma and you all don't care. If John-John and Caroline had a trauma you'd help them but you don't give a damn for black children. Well sir, next thing I know a man is in my room to escort me downstairs to have a fifteen-minute visit with my girls. After that, the next thing was that I was back home. I didn't even go back for the checkup. When I pass that place on the bus I still feel weird.

Whenever any member of our family goes in the hospital we move into the lounge. At all times one of us is there to take care of our sick. My grandmother gets her church members to come and pray. And we do not eat hospital food. I was so hungry when I was in the hospital. Look like I just couldn't get well on that hospital food. Soon as they took them tubes out of me I had Oscar and White bring me some Chinese food from the New Garden on Avenue B. Lillian brought me some good eggplant.

LILLIAN'S EGGPLANT

Peel and slice the eggplant and dip in batter and brown in olive oil. Just light brown on both sides. In another skillet sauté garlic and chopped onions for 5 minutes and add tomatoes, salt and pepper and basil and cook for 15 minutes. In a casserole place alternate layers of eggplant, tomato sauce, mozzarella cheese and grated Parmesan and Romano cheese, finishing off with mozzarella on the top. Dot with butter and bake.

In one way I was glad to be in the hospital. I got a little rest. The day before I went in the hospital I had that dinner party for Rachel Wright and two days before that I was really into something. I had a 2:00 P.M. rehearsal at the Thirteenth Street Theatre for Nat White's play *To Catch a Crooked Crow,* which meant I had to make supper for the girls before I left home. I knew that one of their favorites was

BOEUF AUX NOIX DE PALME
(*Beef with Palm Nuts*)

First boil your nuts. While this is happening salt and pepper and flour 1 pound of stew beef. Brown in palm oil and when just about ready add 2 chopped onions and sauté. Take your nuts off the fire and cool them down. Peel and mash them and strain the juice. Adjust salt and add guinee peppers. Put everything in a pot and cook for 2 hours on simmer. Use enough water to make it have enough gravy to cook soupy. Then add 1 cup of rice.

Note: I get my nuts from my friend Patrice in Kinshasa but as they come canned most fancy food shops don't have them but stores that sell exotic foods sometimes carry them.

Then at 6:00 P.M. I ran uptown to the Renny (Renaissance Ball Room). The New Breed was having a "soul in." I was the commentator for their fashion show and we (Sun Ra and the Solar Myth Science Orkestra) were playing also. Everything was beautiful. Only thing was that I had my Sun Ra outfit on for the New Breed and my New Breed dress on the Sun Ra. But nobody noticed. Everybody was there. Ted Wilson, Russell and Grace, Kane, Larry and Evelyn Neal, Jocelyn, José, Hattie, Leroi and Sylvia and Bill and Cecil and Rap. I'm telling you all the beautiful people except Dorothy and White. Sissy and Mary arrived too late. But we all went to Wells's and hung out till 4 A.M. Sissy and Mary had

WAFFLES AND FRIED CHICKEN

Mix 2 cups sifted cake flour, a pinch salt and 4 teaspoons baking powder together in a bowl and add 2 cups milk. Beat and add ½ cups cold water. Beat some more and then add 1 stick melted butter. Cook on waffle iron and serve with fried chicken.

I had

GRITS AND SCRAMBLED EGGS

Add 1 cup hominy grits to 4 cups cold water and start to cook on a high fire. When it boils turn fire down to simmer and cover and cook for 45 minutes. Stir often with a wooden spoon. Serve with butter or gravy or fried meat. Or grease if that's all you got.

Note: If you use instant grits you still got to cook them for 45 minutes. Only person who can cook regular grits in 10 minutes is Vinie Burrows and she never cooks more than 3 tablespoons at a time. Some people say grits have no nutritional value but Vinie's Gregory is a fine healthy nine-year-old and Vinie cooked grits for him every morning when he was a baby.

We had a good time that morning. Every time I see Mary Greenly I have a good time. She has such good vibrations. John Coltrane was her cousin. He wrote a song for her called "Cousin Mary." I guess beautiful vibrations run in that family. This is

COUSIN MARY
GREENLY'S GREEN SALAD

½ pound raw spinach
handful Bibb (Boston) lettuce
1 small romaine

Mix all the greens together after you have washed and dried them. Make a salad dressing out of 1 part peanut oil and ½ part lemon juice, salt and pepper and powdered garlic. Toss and serve.

Taxis and Poor Man's Mace

Wilson Pickett found him a love and I found me a way . . .
to get a taxi—I use Black Flag roach spray. My heart
has been hurt by taxi drivers. One day Chandra had a fever
and was very sick, I stood on the corner of First Avenue
with her in my arms, in the pouring rain, and I will never
forget that nine taxis passed me. I was only going from Four-
teenth to Twenty-sixth Street.

One time I almost got killed cause I rode on the door from
Houston to Second Street. The driver told my grandmother that
he didn't have to take people like her. We had just had a
wonderful engagement party for her and she was leaving to go
back home. People think taxis just don't want to go to Harlem
but that driver didn't want to take my grandmother to Penn
Station. Well, when he said that, I saw red. I thought of all
the years my grandmother personally had put up with the
whims of white folks and told the driver that this night he
would go to Penn Station or I would go to my grave. He
went. I grabbed the door handle and he pulled off and I
pulled my legs up and I held on. People were screaming and
I held on. I thought of Sam and Dave, just keep holding

on. And I did. He stopped at Second Street and my grandmother got in. He said, "Who do you people think you are?" and I said, "We are."

I think my next book will be the notes of a black woman trying to hail a taxi. Any taxi story you got I can top. This spring I just got fed up. People talking about colored people are late, half the time the reason is that they can't get a taxi.

Anyhow what happened was that I was on my way to AB's house, it was Thanksgiving and we was having a big dinner. Everybody brought a dish. I brought

FEIJODA

1 pound black beans (wash and soak overnight). Next day put the beans and 1 pound Spanish sausages, ½ pound salt pork, 1 smoked tongue (cut in cubes) and 1 pound stew beef in a pot and bring to a boil. After it boils, cover and simmer for 2 hours or until the beans are tender. In a skillet, add ¼ cup palm oil (or use peanut oil) and sauté onions and garlic and about 2 cups beans mashed up and then put all back in the pot and cook for ½ hour more. Some people then take the meat out of the pot and put it on a separate platter, but I leave it all together and serve with rice, collard greens and

THIRD WORLD ONIONS

Take 1 small Bermuda onion
1 large red onion and
1 large yellow onion and slice thin.

Cover with boiling water, then drain, then add salt, Louisiana Hot Sauce, vinegar and palm or peanut oil and marinate for 1 hour.

Back to the taxi. I stood for forty-five minutes and all the taxis were "off duty." The children were so happy. They love parties and they were excited. One taxi pulled right up to us and said he was going to lunch. I said that I only wanted to go across Houston (from Avenue C about six blocks to Elizabeth Street). He said, "Too bad. Take the bus." Now, everybody knows that the phantom bus runs on Houston Street and it takes forever to come.

So I reached my hand in the open window and he started to roll up the window on my arm and called me a nigger bitch and pulled away. In the meantime, Chandra thought that we could get in and she was leaning on the back door so that when he pulled away she fell. My hands were full of food and it was a mess. She was hurt, not physically but inside. She said, "We only want to go to the party, why doesn't that taxi want to take us?" That did it. I made a vow it would be the last time I couldn't get some satisfaction!!!

Now I carry rocks in my purse for the drivers who have closed windows and when I approach a driver with an open window who says he is going to lunch, I take him right out with my poor man's mace.

Work

To tell the truth I ain't never really had no serious job working from nine to five. The ones I had I didn't keep cause my nerves would not take it. It's just not my rhythm . . . not my style. I have had some freakish jobs. I used to sew for a photographer. I made special effects such as aprons for elephants and six-sleeved shirts for a shirt ad. But my cooking jobs were the funniest. I remember "Obedella, Obedella, I want to be your fella!" That's what Jean used to say every time I came to work. Obedella was my new name since I had become the cook in Pee Wee's Slave Trade Kitchen. It didn't last long. But everyone dug my cooking. One of the things that everyone dug was chicken in peanut butter sauce. It is a West African dish sometimes called

GROUND NUT STEW

Cut up and season and sauté the chicken in peanut oil. When brown, add chopped bell pepper and chopped onions. When the onions are transparent, add red pepper and chicken broth and lots chunky-style peanut butter. Sauce should be on the stiff side. Serve with rice or plantain.

Every Friday at Pee Wee's we had a fish fry. One of the favorites was fried croakers. I would buy small croakers and coat with corn meal and fry in peanut oil. I got them every Friday very fresh from Hessey on Avenue C. Sometime he would have catfish and that was the day you could tell who was above or below the Mason-Dixon line. When I would say we have fried catfish all the South Carolina and Georgia, 'Bama and 'Sippi folk would say, "I'll have the

FRIED CATFISH

First off you got to skin the catfish. To skin: draw a sharp knife around the fish in back of the gills and pull off the skin with the pliers. (You can use your hands.) Clean and cut up the catfish and salt and pepper, then pat with corn meal. Fry in very hot grease in your heavy black cast-iron skillet.

Serve with anything—especially

HUSH PUPPIES

Mix corn meal and eggs and salt and buttermilk along with pinch of sugar and fry in deep fat. Serve hot.

Hush puppies are said to have gotten their name from some fishermen who were having a fish fry. The hound dogs were barking and baying at the moon and the one fisherman who

was cooking the corn meal threw several cooked puffs at the
hounds and said, "Hush, puppies." You can believe this if you
believe all the other American folk tales.

I used to roast ribs in the back yard and the neighbors gave
Pee Wee a hard time. I'd made a dish called

OBEDELLA'S BARBECUED SPARERIBS

Parboil the ribs, then marinate the ribs overnight in lemon
juice and salt and pepper. Then brush with your favorite
barbecue sauce and roast on a grill.

and a favorite for people who don't eat swine was

BARBECUED BEEF RIBS
with Avenue A sauce

Parboil the ribs until almost done. Cool and use 1 bottle
barbecue sauce and add chopped-up onions and ½ bottle of
Picka Pepper (dark) Sauce. Let the ribs marinate in this
stuff for an hour. Then place ribs in a shallow pan and cook
in hot oven until done.

Hadi and I were going to do a Latin soul thing together
but we never got around to it. She did help me cook one
day because I was jammed up with work. I was making a kind
of arroz con pollo. Somehow we started talking about Fidel
Castro's visit here and how he shocked the white folks by
bringing his own chickens to that Murray Hill hotel. I don't
think they cared about him going to Harlem . . . the chickens

were the thing. We laughed and laughed and I decided to call the dish

CASTRO CON POLLO

Cut up the chicken in very small pieces. Season with salt and pepper and garlic and brown in olive oil. When brown add fresh parsley (chopped) and rice and chicken broth. Cover and cook slowly until the rice is cooked but not broken open. Adjust seasoning, add capers and olives.

Everyone used to tease me all the time. I was damned if I did and damned if I didn't. If I wore lapas they would say, "Cook is in her African bag today." If I wore Western clothes they would say, "Cook into her white bag today." All kinds of funny things would happen to me. One day I came to work laid out in all my do. I was in my Indian bag that day and you could not tell me that I was not fly. I was so fly that I cooked my Indian bell ring right in the blueberry cobbler. It was a mess. I stood over everyone who ordered blueberry cobbler and waited to see if they would bite into it. It turned up on the plate of an old man who said, "The cook is crazy." He said that it was the last time he would ever eat there.

Most of the time the customers would come back. Jacques Jones would come in every Saturday night just to get a piece of

PECAN PIE

Boil 1 cup sugar with 1½ cups cane or corn syrup for about 3 minutes. Beat 3 eggs and slowly add the syrup mixture.

Add lots of butter and vanilla and about 1½ cups coarsely broken pecan nuts. Turn into unbaked pie shell and bake about 40 minutes.

Another specialty at Pee Wee's was

CHITTERLINGS

People think chitterlings is something only the southern nigras eats but let me tell you about the time I was in this fancy restaurant in Paris and the people said, "Let us order, we know this place." You know the type. They are usually found in Chinese restaurants. Speaking of Chinese restaurants, do you feel foolish looking in the waiter's face and ordering "Beef and Chinese vegetables?" I mean nobody don't. Anyhow back to the French restaurant. So these people order for me and they are just on pins and needles, dying, really dying for me to taste this enjoyable rare dish. Well thank you Jesus the food arrives and it ain't nothing but CHITTERLINGS in the form of a sausage. They call it *andouillette*. Here is a recipe from Bill Larkins when he used to cook at Pee Wee's

CHITTERLINGS A LA LARKINS

    5 pounds chitterlings (frozen)
    3 bay leaves
    3 tablespoons soy sauce
    2 medium-size onions
    1 cup white vinegar
    ½ teaspoon garlic powder or
        3 cloves garlic, minced
    1 tablespoon Worcestershire sauce

1. Let chitterlings thaw completely.
2. Drain and clean.
3. Add 1 cup vinegar and 1 onion, cut up.
4. Let marinate in refrigerator overnight. This will remove some of the odor so that it won't be noticed during cooking.
5. Place on stove in large saucepan or Dutch oven—medium flame.
6. Add bay leaves, garlic and soy sauce.
7. Bring to boil and cook 1½ to 2 hours or until tender.
8. Do not add water to chitterlings. They add their own moistness to pot.
9. Remove from pot after cooked.
10. Cut up into bite-size pieces and place in large skillet.
11. Add enough chitterling broth to cover.
12. Dice onion and add to skillet.
13. Add Worcestershire sauce.
14. Simmer 15 to 20 minutes.
15. Serve immediately.

And

BILL LARKINS' LIMA BEANS AND BAKED BREAST OF LAMB

Baby limas—dry—wash—don't soak.
Smoked pork meat, ham hocks, neck bones.
Water to cover—bay leaf, onions and cloves.
Cook over moderate flame for 2 to 2½ hours.

2 or 3 racks breast of lamb. Wash, dry. Heat oven to 350 degrees. Salt, pepper, add fresh garlic. Place in shallow baking pan, bake for approximately 1 hour until brown and crisp. Pour off grease while baking.

I used to feed people on the side too. Like Stella says, "It ain't nothing but some food." I don't understand how we can live in the richest country in the world and still have so many hungry people. I don't ever have no money to lend, but I can't refuse to give food away. So I would always feed the painters and the musicians and the drunks and anybody that really was hungry. The work was hard but I really dug that brief chapter in my life. I left to go to the New Politics convention in Chicago and the kitchen was closed until René and Bill Larkins took over. I was told that when people asked where that strange cook had gone somebody said, "Gone crazy, black power done run her crazy!"

* * * *

All the jobs I ever had the people have thought that I was weird. When I was about sixteen I had a job as a stock girl in Lit Brothers Department Store. They thought I was weird. I was so involved with my business as president of the Nat King Cole fan club that I couldn't hardly do my work. I had a great big crush on Nat. I wrote to his press agent and got membership cards etc. for my "fan club." The only thing about my fan club was that I was the only permanent member. I let my friends become honorary members and when Nat came to town we made a show. I would let them go with me to that and Nat thought they were the fan club. Honorary members couldn't hold cards. Since I didn't have any meetings etc. now I can't figure out what I did but I remember I used to be very busy. I would bug the disc jockeys to play Nat's tunes and I was even on a couple of radio programs plugging and praising Nat. At work they didn't bug me too much about the fan club but then I got stage-struck and that they found really weird.

This was at the same time that I started studying at the Hedgerow Theatre with Jasper Deeter and Rose Schulman and I was really not very interested in how many of size 9 dresses from Jonathan Logan were on the rack. It was a terrible job anyhow. The salespeople were very insensitive to the stock people. It was the same old story—most of the salespeople were white and most of the stock people black. The saleswomen used to refer to a grown man as the "stock boy." They would ask me to run errands for them. Like, "Get me some coffee hon, O.K.?" Off I would go to get the coffee and I'd come sailing back just as the floor was full of customers, all the dresses off the rack, off the hangers and the buyer screaming, "Where the hell is the stock girl?" This would be a humiliating confrontation. She would say, "Your job is to pick dresses off the floor and keep the racks neat and not to get coffee for other people. Is that clear?" I hated that job. Thank you Jesus, I got my first role on the stage and was able to bear it.

*   *   *   *

The other time in my life when I had a job as a cook was in 1957 at the Hedgerow Theatre. I couldn't make it too tough there as cook either. A company from New York came down for the season and leased the theater. I would have rather had a job as an actress but they weren't doing *The Crucible* that year. I had been studying for several years and I was full of John Dewey and Jasper Deeter and I believed. Not so important what I believed in as that I believed. One thing that I believed in was that old bullshit "talent will out." I studied hard to prepare myself for the theater world. I thought that I would be the "black hope of the American theater." I was young. I studied Chekhov inside and out. I used to picture myself playing Helena in *Uncle Vanya* and secretly pictured myself playing Nina in *The Sea Gull*. I knew that I had it.

Sometimes Jasper would come in and just talk about the inequities of the American way and after class everyone would feel so guilty they would buy me beers in Media.

I remember I used to get the Chester bus to Rose Valley from Media and it was only full of black women who worked out there. They couldn't figure how come I was wearing jeans and sweaters to work. In my most Chekhovian voice I would say, "I'm an actress, not a domestic. I'm on my way to the theater." They would look at me like I was out of my mind. One day I got on and the driver said, "Too hot to scrub floors today, right sweetie?" For some reason I felt depressed. If the black people and the white people couldn't see that I was "the black hope of the American theater," was I?

I worked in the commissary part of the time and took classes part time and ran after Don the other part of the time. It was a scandal. Last interracial scandal they had was when Josh White and Libby Holman walked up Rose Valley Road from the theater to the house holding hands. Some of the people were real, not counting Jasper and Rose. I liked Buck Henry, David, George, Alma and Dick a lot. Recently I saw George and he reminded me of the Mexican pot luck that I used to make. It was a combination of corn, tomatoes, onions, green peppers and ground meat. I would also make spaghetti with sausages and meatballs. And I'd buy wine out of the "budget." That would really flip Dorothy out. I think the whole thing came to a head the night we had wine and toasted garlic bread and Caesar salad and beef stroganoff. With baked Alaska for dessert. We talked it over and agreed that I wasn't cut out to run the commissary. She said that I didn't understand that actors were not supping at Twenty One, they were just getting fed. I didn't. So I was relieved of my duties, and just in time too. My big chance came. They were doing *Streetcar Named Desire* in Bristol and David told them about me and I got the part. Not Blanche but one of the ladies on the stoop. When Blanche arrives at Stella's house, she asks directions and I'm one of those neighbors. I had one line. "Dis is it, honey-o" or something like that. Anyhow what did I care? My first paying job in the theater and I was going to be with a Barrymore . . . Diana Barrymore had the lead.

I was a nervous wreck. Maybe they wouldn't like my projection. Maybe they wouldn't like my delivery. Maybe they wouldn't like my technique. Maybe they wouldn't like me. But they didn't pay me no mind. My little part was so insignificant. By the end of the week I had caused "scandal there too." Everyone had warned me what a bitch Diana Barrymore was, but she was the only person I talked to during the whole week I was there. As a matter of fact, we became friends. We talked about voodoo and vibrations and stuff like that. The scandal I caused was because some apprentice said he saw me in my dressing room on my hands and knees talking in unknown tongues. It was a lie. I was on the floor looking for my shoes and cussing to myself. See, that's what I mean, white and black folks speak a different tongue.

My first part was in a little theater production of *The Wisteria Trees*. My cousin Juanita was staying with us at the time and she had a part as one of the children. I was so stage-struck that I don't even know if it was a good production or not. That I can't remember. It didn't even bother me then to play the role of one of the slaves. I was just happy to be in a play. It is funny that my first role on the stage was a slave and my first Broadway role I played a slave too. I was Big Pearl in *Mandingo*. This time my feelings about slaves were a little different. I did resent it, it was clear that the black actors in the play were overtrained to play those jive slave roles. Work was so scarce that many of the actors didn't even want to deal with that issue, me included. It was at the same time *The Blacks* was playing downtown and there was talk that they were going to picket. I was secretly hoping they would. On the other hand I thought it was my chance and if they did I wouldn't get my "chance" on Broadway.

My chance didn't last long. *Mandingo* got terrible reviews and in two weeks we were closed. The cast included Georgia Burke, Vinie Burrows, Hilda Simms, Cooley Wallace, Fran Bennett, Brooke Haywood (Margaret Sullavan's daughter), Dennis Hopper, Franchot Tone. Franchot talked to me a lot about Hedgerow. Brooke and Dennis got married after the show. Vinie and I became friends and she is now one of my closest. I grew very fond of Georgia and after *Mandingo* didn't see her for a long time. Then in '65 the girls and I were in American Express in Paris and I eyed Georgia on the escalator and at the same time she eyed me. I screamed, "Georgia Georgia" and she screamed, "Big Pearl Big Pearl." Georgia took us all to the Café de la Paix to have refreshments. It was a warm April day and Georgia said, "April in Paris, sipping ice tea at the Café de la Paix." Yeah I said it beats life on the plantation don't it.

I had to laugh when I read a review a few weeks ago about an actress I used to know at the Hedgerow Theatre. She is now a leading young ingénue in the theater. The review gave her *loads of laurels* and said she was a sensitive, imaginative, vital actress. I thought back when we had just come to New York City and used to hang out. She invited me to dinner and first off it was a trauma because she lived in one of those doorman buildings and doormen are notorious for mistaking all black people for servants—and always send us to the service door.

The minute I stepped in her apartment I knew something was wrong. No smells of food cooking or having been cooked. The kitchen was spotless. My daddy always told me that you had to watch those people who never dirtied the kitchen. He said if they don't make a mess in the kitchen they ain't cooking nothing fit to eat. Anyhow we all sat around for a while sipping drinks. I kept wondering where and when was the food. After what seemed hours she said, "Anybody hungry?" And then went to work. She opened a box of frozen peas (in a cellophane buttered pack). A box of instant mashed potatoes and opened a can of chicken (packed in water).

I begged off. I said that I had drank too much and just had to go home and sleep it off. They didn't mind cause you know they didn't want a drunk nigger around to ruin the party. So she asked the doorman to help me get a cab. It wasn't hard because the doorman assured the driver that I wasn't going to Harlem. Soon as I got home I fried a piece of liver and put on a little bit of grits and in a short time I had an epicurean delight.

Speaking of laurels, the popular name of laurel is bay leaf. Laurels have been said to be the symbol of triumph. Hence the expression "to bestow laurels." The Greeks believed that laurel branches would drive away evil spirits. A home with serious illness would hang a laurel branch to drive the evil spirits away. Romans said laurels would purify the air. For my part I use it to cook.

LOVE

I Love Dinner Parties

I love.
I love a lot
of people, places and things.
I love my tribe and my friends.
I love couscous, watermelon, getting up early in the morning,
preachers, rivers, music, presents, persimmons, paris, purple,
pottery, sun ra, sardines and grits, cherokees, robert, paul
laurence dunbar, puerto ricans, sassafras tea, kane, the mediterranean, lace curtains, bustelo coffee, children, getting letters,
turnip greens, silver and. . . .

* * * *

One cold winter night in '68 I saw Leroi Hart Bilbs in Pee
Wee's and he was just back from Paris. He introduced me
to Rachel Wright and we started talking about "soul food"
and we decided to give her a dinner party at my house.
The day of the party I woke up with a tummy ache. I
stayed in bed until noon, hoping it would go away. It didn't

but I managed to cook the dinner and it turned out to be one the best dinners I've ever cooked. We had

> Curried Goat
> Fried Butterfish
> Fried Chicken
> Collard and Turnip Greens
> Baked Sweet Potatoes
> Pecan *and* Sweet Potato Pies

I didn't eat anything. My tummy was still hurting me. But we had a lovely time. Adela and Sunny, Eddie and Kay, some people from England and France that Jocelyn McKissick sent over whom I'd never met. Al Simon, Granchan, Lillian, Ted and Barbara Morgan came too. Rachel never made it. She had to go out of town. The funny thing was everyone said I had a glow that evening and I kept saying that I didn't feel good and the glow they saw was fever. They said I had the glow of health. Eight hours after they left my house I was in the hospital. Some of the same people gave me some recipes. Here's

EDDIE'S MAMA'S PIG'S FEET

> 6 feet, split
> 1 cup vinegar
> 1 onion
> celery tops
> 2 teaspoons salt
> 3 limes
> hot sauce
> 6 peppercorns
> 2 cloves garlic
> 3 bay leaves

4 celery stalks
1 cucumber
1 pimento

Cook feet until they fall apart in water with vinegar, onion,
celery tops and salt. After done, strain the liquid. Remove
bones. Squeeze juice of 3 limes. Add dash of hot sauce.
Add spices. Add thinly sliced celery stalks. 1 cucumber thinly
sliced. Chop 1 small pimento. Put in large tureen and serve
warm in soup bowls.

BAKED LAMB WITH AL SIMON SAUCE

Marinate lamb in minced onions, vinegar and garlic. Baste
often. Bake at approximately 350 degrees. Use meat thermome-
ter to test for doneness—outside should be crisp and inside
pink.

MEATBALLS
à la Barbara Morgan

1 medium onion, chopped
1 tablespoon chopped green pepper
½ cup tomatoes
1 clove garlic, minced
salt
curry powder
peanut oil
½ cup bread crumbs
1 cup milk
1 pound ground meat
1 egg
flour

Sauté onion, green pepper, tomatoes, garlic, salt and curry powder in oil. Add bread crumbs, which have been soaked in milk. Cook until dry. Add all this to the ground meat, mix thoroughly, add egg, shape into balls, roll in flour, fry in deep fat.

* * * *

I really dig cooking and eating with friends. Some of the best times were when I lived on Thirtieth Street and Johnny Mae was still here. We used to really get into it. I liked to have people come by surprise and then figure out how to feed six people on two fish and a loaf of bread. Anyhow, we always ate good. Sometimes people would bring things— anything they had at home or we'd take a collection and buy supplements to my meager "pantry." The combinations were really soulful.

THIRTIETH STREET SOUL BOWL

Brown stew beef and lamb neckbones in flour. Season with salt, pepper and curry. Add water and simmer for 1 hour. Add onions, potatoes, turnips and simmer again. Then add tomatoes. Taste and let simmer for another hour.

... My Friends

I wouldn't take nothing for the friends I got. They are so beautiful. Take Dorothy White. Dorothy can fool the people. They think she is very sane but I'm here to tell you different. But she can cook. Dorothy can take anything and turn it into something else. Dorothy was the one who hipped me on how to prepare myself before eating at white folks' houses. They invite you to dinner and when you get there at 8:00 P.M. (which is already much too late to eat) they act surprised to see you and start giving you a bunch of whisky. I think it is so you can act the fool (everybody knows about niggers and Indians and firewater). Around about 10:00 they start asking in a weird voice, "Anybody hungry?" By that time you so drunk and hungry that you don't even feel like eating. So Dorothy says before you leave home on such an occasion eat some collards and rice. Dorothy wouldn't give me none of her recipes. So I used mine and called them

LAMB LOAF A LA DOROTHY WHITE

If you have a blender use it. If you don't, use a bowl and mix by hand, make sure you mix very well.

Mix a bit of:

> coconut, freshly grated
> peanuts
> egg
> fresh parsley
> scallions

with about 2 cups rice and blend well. Season with salt and pepper. Add that mixture to ground lamb and bake like any other meat loaf.

And

MEAT LOAF A LA WILLIAM WHITE

In a bowl mix onions, bread crumbs (whole wheat), salt and pepper, eggs and curry powder. Blend well together, then add ground beef and small can of evaporated milk and mix together well. Shape into balls. Brown the balls in a butter and oil mixture. Cook for about 15 minutes and then remove the balls and make a pan gravy. Put the balls in the gravy and cook on simmer for 15 more minutes.

Sometimes substitute allspice instead of the curry powder.

Another friend, Louis Gossett, was my acting teacher for a minute. We had a workshop group that was dynamite. It was full of very talented black actors. Yvette Hawkins, Jim Sprull, Ernestine Johnson, Miss Stella Beck, Gyland Kane, Peggy Kirkpatrick, Marie Lucas, Ernie McClintock and Roland, among them.

Louis got an OEO grant during the summer of '66 and we did a bit of traveling around the city parks and centers. Our biggest reception was in Tompkins Park. And it had nothing to do with the community being more theater conscious. It had to do with my public relations people, Kali and Chandra. They went around spreading the word, "My mommy is going to be in a show in the park tonight." Plus the fact that it is our neighborhood and I knew most of the children around the sandbox. When we arrived, the park was full. Mostly kids. We did a series of improvisations and the audience would help "write" the plot and then we would act it out, never knowing how it would end. When my first entrance came there was much applause and catcalls. "Hi Verta," "Ooh, Kali your Mommie's on the stage," "Ooh, look at Kali's mama," "Hello Miss Verta." It was beautiful. I did a Helen Hayes for days. We had a lot of fun that night. Afterward we had a supper party at my house. Barbecued chicken wings, black-eyes, fried chicken, red rice, ham hocks (cooked whole), crackling bread, potato salad, pecan pie, sweet potato pie and watermelon. Besides the cast, Mary Greenly came, Barbara Carter, Ya Ya, Dorothy, Jay, Oscar Jones, and most of the friends of the producer's. Only person who wasn't there was O.W. and we kept thinking that he would show up every minute. Very soon after the GADA (Gossett Academy of Dramatic Arts) party I moved downstairs in the garden apartment. I was determined to try my black thumb. But I just couldn't seem to get nothing to grow. The collard greens wouldn't sprout at all. And the flowers never bloomed. I like fresh flowers and whenever I can I keep a bunch in the kitchen. The food smells mixed with the flower smells is very pleasant. I spend many hours in the kitchen so everything is jammed in it. Books, records, sewing, and company always sit in the kitchen. Considering how small my kitchen is—it is no wonder sometimes I can't find the stove. Back to flowers. I keep them a long time and when they dry out I crush them for sachet bags. The garden is fun. The view is not very hip, but each morning we can rise and walk out into the garden and partake of the polluted air.

We have had some good parties in the garden. Some beautiful people have walked through. One of the best times was last summer when we had a fund-raising fish fry for SNCC. We set up separate tables and put flowers and candles on each table. I was worried because usually my neighbors complained about the noise. But for the first time they didn't. The party was just around the time that SNCC had announced a merger with the Black Panthers. During the day someone mentioned it and then Kali went around telling all the neighbors that we were having a party for the Black Panthers. It was the first time nobody complained about the noise. All the neighbors bought dinners, too. The menu was greens, potato salad and fried whities.

Cynthia Belgrave Farris is my next-door neighbor. She is an actress and a producer. She and her husband produced *Brother Jerro* and *The Strong Breed* by Nigerian playwright Wole Soyinka (who at the time was still in jail on a charge of giving aid to the Biafran rebels). Cynthia was in the original company of *The Blacks,* too. Her mother fries the best fish. She takes butterfish (or porgies, sea bass or cod) and soaks it for several hours in fresh lime juice, salt, pepper and thinly sliced onions. Then she coats it with flour and fries it in butter. Another Cynthia favorite is steamed codfish steaks. Steam the cod in a shallow pan with lots of lemon juice and butter. Make sure you have a tight-fitting cover and do not overcook. Cynthia serves the steamed cod with something she calls turn corn or cou cou. Depends if she feels like being from Boston or Barbados.

COU COU OR TURN CORN

Bring to a boil ½ cup sliced gombo
1 pint water
salt
Mix ½ cup water with 1 cup corn meal
Add gombo and its water (reserving ½ cup) to corn meal paste.

Stir corn over moderate heat until it thickens; add ½ cup okra water leaving wooden spoon or cou cou stick in mixture. Cook over low heat till done; spoon will come out clean. Mixture should be smooth but not pasty to taste. It should be able to hold its shape when tossed in a warm butter bowl and unmolded.

CORN MEAL POP
another kind of cou cou

1 cup sweet milk
1 cup boiling water
stick cinnamon
1 cup corn meal
¼ cup sugar
1 teaspoon salt
1 teaspoon butter
¼ cup raisins

Bring to boil milk with water and cinnamon. Add corn meal, sugar, salt and butter. Boil directly over fire, stirring constantly until mixture begins to thicken. Remove to top of double boiler, add raisins and allow to steam for 15 to 20 minutes.

I got a friend who won't eat no white bread, drink white milk, won't use no white flour or white pepper. She only uses black pepper, drinks only blackberry wine, black coffee, chocolate milk, eats chocolate cake, black beans, black bread. She says it is because she is so fed up with black being used in a negative sense, that is to say blackheads, blackball, black list, black out, the black plague, blackhearted. Last time I was at her house she made a delicious

STEAK WITH BEAUTIFUL BLACK SAUCE

Sprinkle the sides of each steak with ground pepper. Let stand for 1 hour. Brush your black skillet with beef suet and heat the skillet. Cook the steaks to your desire and remove steaks to a platter and add butter to the skillet and cook butter until it almost is black. Pour butter over the steaks and serve.

A good cooking friend of mine is a dude named René L'Aimont. He is not French; he is colored as you can get. René is from North Carolina. He is an excellent cook. I've had some wonderful meals at his house. The only time I know of that he faltered was when he cooked a pot of chitlins (fifteen pounds) and put in liquid soap—by mistake of course. One thing that René makes very well is

L'AIMONT JAMBALAYA

Fry streak of lean (diced). After it has fried hard add minced garlic and chopped onions until they are brown. Add fresh quartered tomatoes and let the whole thing cook for 10 minutes. Then remove to a big saucepan. Wash the skillet and sauté chicken wings until they are brown. When brown, throw them in the big saucepan. Add butter to the skillet and sauté more onions and peeled shrimp and more garlic. When the onions are brown, dump the whole mess into the big saucepan. Adjust salt and pepper. Cook everything together for 45 minutes. Then adjust seasoning (salt, pepper and cayenne). Add maize and gombos and halved crabs. Cook for another 20 minutes. Serve over rice.

Another friend is thinking of changing his first name. His name is Honky. He is a black man and it gets kind of embarrassing. He is a excellent cook. He used to visit us all the time on Thirtieth Street. We moved and we don't see him too much now. I miss him; he knew lots of ways to prepare cheap meals. One of the most delicious was . . .

STUFFED HEART HONKY STYLE

Slit the heart and remove any gristle and fat and other weird-looking vessels of blood. Fill with soul dressing. Sew up. Then salt and pepper the heart and sauté in peanut oil until it is nearly beautiful black and then cover with tomato juice and beef broth mixed together. Simmer in a covered saucepan until it is tender and breaks easily.

SOUL STUFFING

Crumble 1 hoecake of bread. Add chopped onions, bell pepper, salt and black pepper, a pinch of sage and a little bit of beef broth to hold it together. Mix together and put in honky heart.

Charles Lloyd makes beautiful music. He's so fine that when I met him for the first time I had a straight up love attack. In Paris I could make the best quiche on Rue des Ursulines but when Charles came into my kitchen that day and I was making quiche Lorraine, I made another kind of quiche. Delicious

QUICHE LLOYD

1 cup grated Swiss cheese
4 eggs
pinch salt
pinch nutmeg
¾ cup thin cream
pinch cayenne

Pour cheese into a cream cheese piecrust and add the rest of the stuff above (all mixed together). Bake for 40 minutes in a moderate oven.

ATTENTION: Do not overbake. Stick a silver knife in the center and if it comes out clean—*Voila!* You got it.

I got all kinds of friends—post-office workers, painters, actors, musicians, mothers, fathers, drunks, preachers and poets like Roland Snellings who asked for some vegetarian dishes so here are two for Roland and Ayischia:

BAKED SQUASH

Cut squash in half and take out the membranes and the seeds. Sprinkle inside with salt and pepper, honey and mace. Then spread a taste of honey and dot with butter and top with sesame seeds. Wrap in tinfoil and bake in a hot oven for about 45 minutes. Then remove the foil—stick under the broiler for a hot minute if the squash is not brown.

ONION PIE

This is an onion pie that is similar to Quiche Lloyd.

Sauté 3 large onions in skillet. I use ½ butter and ½ peanut oil. When the onions become translucent sprinkle 2 tablespoons flour on them and sauté for 3 minutes. Then add ¾ cup light cream and add 3 well-beaten eggs and pour everything into a pastry shell. Bake for 45 minutes in hot oven.

. . . African Clothes

I love to wear African clothes. I think I look better in them. But it seems to bother white folks. I remember two incidents where white folks went crazy cause I was dressed in my do. The first time was when the children traveled down south by themselves. It was a real occasion. We had a big lunch with Dorothy and Roland Nelson and Oscar. Then we headed out to Newark to get the plane. The girls were excited and everything was cool until we reached the ticket counter. The woman seemed surprised to find out that we were black. But she was cool. She asked me are THESE the girls who are traveling alone? I said yes. She said, "Why don't you all have some refreshments?" So we went into the restaurant bar and Dorothy and Oscar and Ronald and I had double vodka martinis and the girls had ginger ale. Everybody in there kept looking at us real funny too. They kept staring at the butterfly net and our shoe-box lunches. When we went back to the ticket counter she kept asking if I was sure that John Owen Ritter (Uncle Bubba) would meet them. I told her of course I was sure cause as a matter of fact it took longer to get

from Fairfax to Columbia than from New York City to Columbia by plane and I had just called down south and Aunt
Hattie said Uncle Bubba, Cousin Blanche and Uncle Simmie and Cousin Iva and Miss Belle and Juanita and Jerry
and John and Brenda and Lois and Sister had already left
for Columbia. They were all excited because it was their first
time visiting the airport. It was our first time coming south
in a plane so everyone wanted to visit the airport. It was
only recently that colored folks started using the airport. The
plane was late and over the loud-speaker they paged Uncle
Bubba, Mr. John Owen Ritter, to let him know that the plane
was late. Uncle Bubba said it made him nervous. Only recently white folks in the south started calling black folks Mr.
and Mrs. Some of them still don't.

Once in New York as Dorothy and I were walking in the
Port Authority terminal a woman came running up to me and
started preaching and shouting and just acting like a nut. She
was yelling, "Who do you think you are? What do you people
want? Are you trying to make me a victim of the people
in Harlem? Why do you have on those clothes? You are an
American. You aren't African. Join the Pepsi generation."
   The other time somebody went crazy was at the Sorbonne
when I was helping Julia sell the *pouvoir noir* material in the
stall in the courtyard. It was during the occupation in '68.
The whole courtyard was bustling. Everybody was selling
everything. The Marxists were selling their stuff. The Jeune
Nation was selling their propaganda. People were making
speeches on the loud-speaker. They even had some Africans
selling Billy Graham Bibles. Lena Horne was singing "Now"
on record, coming out of another loud-speaker. One guy was
walking around with a sword tied on his hip and a baseball
bat in one hand and a transistor radio in the other with a
loaf of bread under his arm. I had on all my do and was

feeling very good because I had been speaking only French all day and was able to talk to a lot of the brothers and sisters of the Third World who didn't speak English.

I was sitting there minding my own business when I hear this cracker voice say, "Do you speak English?" and I said, "I "I sho do honey." "Well why are you wearing those African clothes, you are a Negro." I said, "I am who I think I am." "I am free and free to define myself." "No you are not. You are a Negro. You are of American descent. I'm from Georgia and have spent all my life with Negroes and had a black mammy when I was a child." So I got mad and said, "So did I."

Now I have done a lot of research on food and found out that Long Island ducks are not from Long Island at all. They are the descendants of ducks imported from Peking around 1870. Georgia peaches are descendants of peaches brought from China. Potatoes are native to South America and were taken to Europe by the Spanish explorers "when they discovered South America." They discovered "Indians and potatoes and squash and peppers and turkeys and tomatoes and corn and chocolate." They took everything back to Europe except the Indians. The settlers who later came from Europe brought the descendants of these vegetables to North America. Now, if a squash and a potato and a duck and a pepper can grow and look like their ancestors, I know damn well that I can walk around dressed like mine.

... Bon Voyage Parties

I love bon voyage parties. One year I had one planned on the *Leonardo da Vinci.* I was going to have this big "bon voyage," invite all my friends and when they cried and said how sorry they were that I was leaving, I'd leave, too. Truth being that I wasn't planning to really leave since I didn't have a ticket anyhow. I just wanted to have a different kind of party—but I told so many people of my plot that nobody came. Reminds me of the guy I met in London who asked me, "How come you people always getting arrested on alleged plots?"

But we did have a bon voyage party that March day we left the country "for good!!" That was some party. Seventy-five adults, forty-five children. We had the whole lounge. I thought that I would be out of the country for good so I invited EVERYBODY! Black folks, white folks, the man from the candy store on Third Street, militants, Uncle Toms, racists, Black Nationalists, Yorubas, hustlers, gamblers, actors, writers, husbands, wives, ex-husbands, ex-wives, mistresses and ex-mistresses and so on. I figured since I was leaving that they would have it. Well, the party was a smash!! They all showed up and some brought their friends. Everybody brought something. White brought three bottles of Half and Half. Bob Stocking brought a bottle of gin and his camera but he forgot his film.

Vinie brought oatmeal cookies

VINIE'S OATMEAL COOKIES

Cream 1 cup butter and 1 cup sugar. Add 2 beaten eggs and 2 cups flour, 2 cups oatmeal, 1 teaspoon baking powder, pinch salt and some cinnamon, raisins and some chopped nuts. Mix together and add enough milk to make a stiff dough. Then drop on a buttered cooky sheet 1 inch apart.

Bake in hot oven for 8 to 10 minutes.

And Bernard Boston brought Gypsy Rose.
    André brought champagne.
    C⚔ and China brought some sweet wine.
    Gregory brought Coke and ginger ale (for the children).
    David brought a bottle of Jack Daniel's.
    Oscar brought a gallon of Gallo.

I just can't remember—we had so much stuff that I sent it back with everybody and told them to have a party.

Mrs. Jackson was going to bring some sweet potato pies but Johnnie Mae thought that would be too colored. As a matter of fact Mrs. Jackson was going to give us a couple of shoe box lunches but Johnnie Mae said that would definitely be too too colored. Mrs. Jackson can cook chocolate cake—Lord she can cook chocolate cake.

MRS. JACKSON'S CHOCOLATE CAKE

Sift 2 cups flour and 2 cups sugar, 1 teaspoon salt together. Add 2 sticks butter and mix with finger tips or pastry blender. Add melted chocolate to the mixture. Place in the icebox overnight. Next morning, add 3 well-beaten eggs, 2 teaspoons vanilla and 2 teaspoons baking powder. Bake in 9-inch baking pans in a moderate oven for 35 minutes.

Cover with a chocolate butter frosting made with 1 stick butter and 1 cup Four X sugar, vanilla and 1 ounce melted chocolate.

She also used to make wine. She'd get the berries from somewhere in Central Park and this is how she told me she would do.

MRS. JACKSON'S WINE

Gather your berries where you can and fill a large stone jar with the ripe berries. Cover with water and tie a cloth over the jar and let stand for 4 days to ferment. Then mash and press berries through a cloth. To every gallon of berry juice add 2 pounds sugar—1 brown and 1 white.

Put the mixture back in stone jar. Cover and close.
For 9 days skim each morning.
Skim each morning for the next 9 days or until it clears.
When clear, carefully pour into another vessel.
Cork tightly and put in a cool place for 3 months.

We had flowers and candies and fruits. Barbara Carter arrived just as they were ready to sail but they waited for her to come aboard. She gave us a jar of hair grease, Sulphur 8, a hard thing to find in Europe, a drawing from Vigo. The whistle sounded, Chandra and Kali started to cry and I was wailing, and we all were hugging and kissing and falling out. We set sail and waved good-by to fun city.

Everyone on the pier was waving and crying and yelling and throwing kisses and then all of a sudden they started disappearing one at a time. Bob Stocking was acting weird. He was gesturing with his fist all clenched and jumping up and down. I didn't know what the hell was going on and it was a few years before the black power fist was popular. So I keep on waving and throwing up my fist too. The mystery was solved the very next morning. I called Johnnie Mae from the ship to see if I had left a missing bag in her car, since she and Fred had driven us to the pier.

Johnnie Mae started screaming. "Child, you should have been on the pier yesterday after you left. Lord, it was a straight-up race riot." She said that Dean was standing on a car bumper trying to see over Fred's back and a white man wearing a black suit, a rifle tie pin in his red tie and an American flag in his lapel said, "Get off that car." Dean said, "Is it your car?" "No, but I know you people—you have no respect for other people's property and you smell bad and you don't want to go to the war in Vietnam either." Well, child, that was it! Dean said, "Here, Vinie, take Sojourner [then a four-month-old baby]." Vinie said, "No, dear, no." Dean said, "Woman, I said take the girl, I got to fight." She did. While this was happening, Oscar spit on the flag in his lapel. Then the man walked away to get some of his friends. Oscar and Dean and Johnnie Mae organized. That's the reason I saw them leaving one at a time. Anyhow, the man and his troops lined up and came back to fight. Oscar and Dean took the offensive and before you could say "John Birch," the manure hit the fan and Johnnie Mae says all she remembers when she was holding the man down on the ground is that she thought Oscar had put out one of his eyes. But Dean says that was the friend of the guy in the black suit that she was holding and that it wasn't Oscar it was Sol who was punching him. Johnnie Mae says it's all blurred cause they all looked alike. Anyhow, they made a hasty retreat and Johnnie Mae says she heard his wife say, "George, I told you not to discuss politics up here."

The boat ride was very restful. After our big bon voyage party I needed to rest. The children went to the ship's nursery all day so I rested between meals on my deck chair. We had the early breakfast sitting at 8:00 A.M. and at 11:00 A.M. I had my bouillon on my deck chair. Lunch was at noon and at 4:00 P.M. I had tea in my deck chair and dinner at 6:00 P.M. I did a lot of reading. Nothing much else. The people were not too friendly and them that were were not on my wave length so I was sort of the mystery lady of the ship. Someone said I was African. Someone said I was from the Fiji Islands. Someone said I couldn't speak English.

But in due time the origin of the "mystery lady" was apparent. It turned out that the lady that "George" came to see acted up with me and I had to go into my act. What happened was that a few days before we were to dock at the first port, Cobh, Ireland, there was a children's party in the main lounge. The children sat around on little chairs in a semicircle in front of the tables where the adults sat. A nice lady would ask who wanted to sing or dance or just do their thing. My children were sitting a little ways from me and weren't participating. All of a sudden I hear a voice singing, "Don't You Let Nobody Turn You Around" and there is Chandra at the microphone singing for days. She was funny because you couldn't understand the words and she didn't know the right tune but she was singing from the heart. When she finally finished there was much applause. She bowed and they applauded and she bowed again. This went on for a while and it was really funny. Then she sat down in another seat from the one she had at first. A lovely Indonesian lady tapped me on the shoulder to tell me what a nice child I had and I started beaming and we started talking women talk. Then out of a corner of my ear I heard, "Yes, because if the mother won't do anything about it I will." So in my best Chekhovian voice I said, "Madame, if you please, that is my daughter. She is three years old. She is not at all accustomed to being spoken to in that manner. If there is a problem, ask me. I am her mother and I will deal with you. But please, madame, do not bully my daughter." She said, "Oh you shut up. There are some people who don't want you on this boat anyhow. When you start acting and talking like white folks then I'll listen to you." Well I did a change up on her and in my best Geechee voice I said, "Lady, I am going to throw you overboard today—today. If God gives me strength this day, today today. You will swim to Cobh in Ireland." So, I turned over three tables to reach her and just as I had my arm outstretched and was winding it up some old man with white hair and a white mustache said, "Don't let her sink you to her level. Ignore her." I hit him with my purse and said, "You don't know the levels I can sink so get out of my face." By this time the lounge was in an uproar. The nice lady had the children singing the Dutch national anthem and the stewards were just giving out drinks to the adults and I decided that I'd cool it for a minute. They had put the tables back so I went to sit down and I told the lady I would wait until she left and I would throw her overboard without a big scene. I sipped my rum and coke and waited. Every time she would start to rise I would ask, "Are you ready" and she would sit again. After a while it was obvious she was scared.

Then the main man came to find out what had happened and she ran up to him and said, "Thank God you've rescued me." He asked what happened and she said, "These negroes are oversensitive. All I said to her was that she was not wanted on the boat and that when she became white we would accept her. Don't listen to anything she says. Look into my eyes and you can see I am telling the truth. Now please walk me to my stateroom—I want to get ready for dinner." The main man looked at her and at me, then he walked her to her stateroom. Later he came to my stateroom to offer the apologies of the Holland-American Line. He said, "Believe me, everyone wants you on the boat. We are terribly sorry, etc, etc." The old lady had had the same meal sitting as us but—she changed up. After that she kind of cooled it and wasn't around too much.

But I knew how to cool her out. Every time I passed her I would say, "I put a spell on you and you have six more months." And once in the lounge I came with my sewing. I just sat and sipped rum and coke and sewed. I had a bunch of pins and cotton, and people asked me what was I doing. I said, "I'm making a doll." They would turn red and walk away. Just as I thought, the new rumor was that I had made a voodoo doll of the lady. By the time we got to Cobh she looked awful. By the time we got to Southampton she looked real bad. By the time we got to Le Havre we got off and by the time she got to Rotterdam. . . .

MIXED BAG

Collards and Other Greens

Collard greens according to the *National Geographic* are prehistoric. The Romans took them to France and England. The Romans are said to have considered them a delicacy. I know I consider them a delicacy. They are very rich in minerals and vitamins. They are biennials.

Speaking of biennials I was at the Biennale in Venice last year. It was a real mess. The Italians were having a lightweight revolt. Like the French were doing in Paris. There was a lot of opposition to the Biennale. A lot of painters didn't want to show and turned their canvas to the wall and covered the sculpture. A few pavilions didn't open and the Danish students occupied the Swedish pavilion. The Russian pavilion wasn't finished and people couldn't tell what side they were on, if they had been open. Cyprus painters wouldn't go in or show in the Greek pavilion. And I thought of not going in the United States pavilion. The only black painters in the show was an African project that some European in the bush somewhere teach Africans to paint like Europeans. Everyone loved the pieces but they didn't win any prizes. The United

States pavilion didn't have one black painter in the show and when I asked a famous New York City gallery owner why, he said that Bob Thompson had died the year before.

The Venetians kept screaming, "Oh! Carmen Jones" every time I would walk down the street. Every time I passed a gondolier he would get a dirty look on his face and push out his pelvis and shout gondola, gondola. One cat came running out of a shop as I went past and yelled, "Carmen Jones, Carmen Jones." I don't hardly look like Dorothy Dandridge. Europeans have some weird ideas about black women.

The Venetian women were the worst. They just out and out laughed. It was funny to them to see something in the shape of a woman but with a black skin. You know how people laugh (uncomfortably most of the time) at chimpanzees.

It was awful. One woman brought her child up to me and asked me to touch the child. I told the waiter who spoke English to tell her if she didn't get out of my face I would slap her and the little brat. Even the ones who went around yelling, "Oh que bella que bella" were not flattering. They weren't admiring me—I was just an exotic freak to them. At the time there was a bunch of Ethiopians in Venice and for some reason they didn't cause a row. Later in Rome I found a way to get a little anonymity. I never wore Western clothes. They were very respectful to me with my African clothes but if I was on the street in Western do, they were impossible. I got to the point where I resented having to pay money for cafés or restaurants. From the extra business they got with me as the side show, I felt that they should have let me eat free.

I didn't hang too long in Italy. I just couldn't take it. In Rome there's a bunch of black people and a bunch of them liked the kind of attention that they were getting. I didn't so I left. I was only there a few days—in that time I met a few sincere people. In general though it is a city full of international never-was-in-the-movies or could-have-been-stars-in-the-movies insincere people. Probably a cultural hangover from their Roman ancestors.

* * * *

Back to collards. I have to take the A train to Harlem to buy my collard greens. They got them on Avenue D but I stopped buying them there because when I was a child I remember at the greens store on Ridge Avenue that when you bought greens, the black man weighed and wrapped them but the white one took the money. It was a put down! I would hear my father talking about it and he'd say that it was one of the ways that they had of keeping black men from feeling like men.

I had forgotten about that until one day last summer, it happened on Avenue D. The Puerto Rican man weighed and wrapped the greens and the white man said that will be fifty-five cents. We argued about that. I said that was robbery. He said it was because they were out of season. I said, "Mister, collard greens ain't never out of season for black folks." But I got to have greens every other day so I gave the Puerto Rican man a dollar and he went inside and came out and started to wait on another customer. I asked for my change and he told me that the man would give it to me. He said, "I'm not in charge of the money." Suddenly I remembered Ridge Avenue and I said that I wanted my money back. He asked me how come and I told him about Ridge Avenue and told him that I was going to organize a boycott of his store and he said he was going to call Bellevue for me. I just couldn't get over it, so I take the A train to buy my greens.

Collard greens almost caused me and Archie Shepp to break friendship. His play was being presented at the Chelsea Theatre and for the opening night party they were going to have a "soul food party." They asked me to cook the greens. Peggy and I cut up fifteen pounds of greens. We got calluses on our fingers. I called a friend of mine (an actor in the play) to ask him to drive me to the theater, and he said, "Didn't they tell you the show is not opening tonight? It's opening Thursday." Well, I better skip the rest and tell you how to make . . .

COLLARD GREENS A LA SHEPP

Have the meat boiling when you clean the greens. Then put the cleaned and cut-up greens in when the meat is just about done. Add salt, pepper, a bit of hot sauce and a bit of sugar. Cook on high for 15 minutes, stirring often. Turn off and let cool, stirring often while it is cooling. I find this is the best way to cook greens. They cook while they are cooling and don't get mushy.

TO CLEAN GREENS

First pick the greens. That is, separate each leaf from the stalk. Pick out the yellow or discolored or weird-looking leaves and remove the tough stems. Take each leaf and shake it (for bugs). Then wash the leaves three times or until there is no more grit. Then you fold each leaf in half and then roll as for a jelly roll, then with a knife or scissors you cut them up.

Note about cooking greens: Greens contrary to popular belief don't have to be cooked all day. Always cook greens in enough water to cover. Some people add a little vinegar to the pot likker. Corn bread with pot likker is delicious.

GREENS OTHER THAN COLLARDS

KALE Very good. Cook the same as collards. Try mixing kale and cabbage together.

MUSTARD Delicious. Mustards are bitter, so add a pinch of sugar. Mix mustards with collards or turnips.

RAPE SALAT I remember Mother Dear used to make this at least once a week. Very delicious. Cook same as other greens.

SPINACH We didn't eat too much of it until recently. You don't need water to cook spinach. Spinach must be washed very carefully as there is much sand and grit in it. On all these greens of course, I am assuming that you are using FRESH GREENS, NOT FROZEN. I only use frozen greens if it is impossible to get fresh. I mean it ain't a way of life. Frozen are still better than the canned greens. A good spinach recipe is to fry the spinach in peanut oil and add a little butter and sprinkle with powdered garlic.

POKE SALAT Cook like quickly in very little water.

ATTENTION: THE ROOTS AND LOWER STALKS OF POKEWEED ARE POISONOUS.

CRESSES SALAT Take the water cress and wash thoroughly. Put in saucepan and pour hot grease over the water cress. Cover with a tight cover and cook for a hot minute.

TURNIPS Cook like collards but not as long a time. I use the roots and tops. Turnips are delicious mixed with other greens.

BEET TOPS Can be cooked with little or no water. Cook very quickly. They are delicious.

DANDELION *See* Cresses Salat

CHARD Cook until tender and then add lots of butter and serve.

PORK CHOP AND CRESSES SALAT

Fry pork chops in skillet until they are dark brown. Then add peppercorns and beef stock and smother until done. When done add water cress and cook for about 8 minutes. Serve with rice.

Poultices and Home Remedies

PLANTAIN LEAVES poultice is good for boils.

PERSIMMON BARK soaked in water is good for diarrhea.

FATBACK placed on sores for three days and two nights promotes healing.

NIGHTSHADE PLANT LEAVES poultice also promotes healing of sores. Leave the nightshade plant leaf poultice on for one day and one night.

A DROP OF TURPENTINE and a drop of camphor and a drop of kerosene and sugar taken for four mornings and three nights will cure a cold.

BROWN PAPER poultice soaked in vinegar is good for soreness and bruises.

SPIRITS OF AMMONIA and water are excellent for upset stomach.

CIGAR ASHES a dental tip from an eighty-five-year-old lady who uses them to brush her teeth.

MUSTARD POULTICE is good for boils and risings. It will draw them to a head.

CLAY AND CHEWING TOBACCO poultice is for insect bites and stings.

EARWAX for cold sores. The earwax used does not have to be your own.

VINEGAR and baking soda paste for mosquito bites.

ASSAFOETIDA AND CAMPHOR BALLS in a little bag around the neck will ward off disease.

NOSEBLEED Catch the blood on a piece of brown paper and burn the paper to stop the nosebleed.

FOR RISING AND KERNELS UNDER THE ARM AND BETWEEN THE LEGS Make a cross with a knife and mark it with soot.

FOR MINOR BURNS Cover area with strips of cellophane tape. Tape will ease pain and draw fire out.

SICKLY BABIES A bottle of pot likker twice a day.

Spices

I use a lot of spices. The ones I use most are . . .

CORIANDER is used in breads, cakes, on pork and is good on baked apples. Said to have been growing in the gardens of Babylon—so be cool.

SAFFRON to me is expensive and overrated. Necessary to make paella and saffron rice.

GARLIC I love. I use plenty of it. The Romans and Greeks believed if you ate a clove a day it would prevent diseases. Garlic juice mixed with honey is said to be good for asthma. Gets rid of worms and I suspect if you use too much it will get rid of more than that.

ALLSPICE I use in stews. Good with cooked fruits. Remember a little bit goes a long way.

POWDERED CAYENNE I never buy. I crush whole guinee peppers and use like cayenne.

CINNAMON Good for coffee, hot chocolate, apple sauce and butter and anything else you'd use cloves for.

MACE Is part of the nutmeg nut and not the kind police use to control "riots." Use mace when you can't decide if you want to use cinnamon or nutmeg.

NUTMEG Always use whole and grate yourself.

PAPRIKA is not just a coloring but contains vitamins and has its own delicate flavor.

PARSLEY Always try to use fresh and not just to decorate.

PEPPERCORNS I always use whole peppercorns and a pepper grinder at the table. It smells and tastes so much better than powdered black pepper.

THYME .... I try always to keep some on hand.

Aphrodisiacal Foods

There are some foods that have an aphrodisiacal nature but you can't be no fool about it. I mean you got to know what you're doing and who you're doing it to. Certain foods blended with herbs and roots can most certainly have a stimulating effect on the sex glands but I'm afraid that it would be most unwise for me to run it down here for several reasons:

1. If it didn't work folks would be mad and blame me.

2. It could work and lead to trouble. Folks would still be mad and blame me.

3. The information is so hip that I'm sure I'd be put on the House Un-American Activities subversive list.

Cocktails and Other Beverages

COCKTAILS

I don't drink cocktails and the only one I know how to make
is a *molotov* and I'd be a fool to give the recipe here.

SWEETEN WATER

Mix syrup in water about a teaspoon to a glass.

LEMONADE

The best lemonade I ever had was when Aunt Virter used to
live on Master Street. She and Uncle Will Ed used to go to
the spring in Fairmount Park in Philadelphia to get their water.
She would make lemonade with spring water and fresh juicy
lemons. I tried it with bottled water and it wasn't as good as
hers, but better than with tap water.

COFFEE

Is said to be a native of Ethiopia. Coffee should always be made in a clean pot. Coffee should always be made with fresh cold water. If you take milk and sugar . . . put the sugar in the cup first and heat (never boil) the milk.

TURKISH COFFEE

In a Turkish coffeepot bring to a boil 1 cup water, 2 teaspoons sugar. Then pour off about ½ cup (save it). Add 2 teaspoons Turkish coffee and cardamom seeds (2 or 3). Let come to a boil and tap the pot gently 3 times. Repeat 3 times. On the third boil add the water you poured off. Serve in demitasse cups.

IRISH COFFEE

Add some whisky.

THIRD WORLD COFFEE

A cinnamon stick, a few cloves, a little orange and lemon peel, sugar and cognac. Light it and slowly add the coffee.

Note on coffee: I find Bustelo and Jamaica Blue Mountain coffees to be the best. Try to get an electric coffee grinder and grind the roasted beans fresh each time. Remember the lighter the roast the stronger the coffee.

TEAS

Some herb teas only have to be steeped. Others you must let boil. Judge by taste—not color. I'm talking about herbs, of course, nothing personal intended.

Honey is the best sweetener. Never buy processed honey. And never heat it; heat kills the vitamin content.

DANDELION root is a natural coffee substitute. The leaves can be used in a raw salad or cooked. Dandelion juice is said to be good for gout and rheumatism.

BERGAMOT is more than hair grease. The leaves and flowers can be used in salads. Leaves added to other teas give a very delicate flavor.

CAMOMILE is good for nervous conditions. I drink it every morning when I am getting the children off to school. Also said to promote menses.

CATNIP is said to relieve pain and recommended for colds.

COUCH GRASS is good for gout; not for cooking.

HOREHOUND is very bitter, good for colds; use honey to sweeten.

GROUND IVY also very bitter; combined with camomile is said to be good for indigestion. Mixed with camomile flower makes an excellent poultice for abscesses.

FEVERFEW is bitter but will calm nerves, get rid of worms and promote the menses.

DILL WATER is good for upset stomachs in children.

TANSY cures children of their worms.

GINGER is good as tea or beer. The tea can be made of crushed roots or ground. Good to relieve cramps and promote the menses. Crush the roots or use ground ginger for tea. The root can also be used in many meat and poultry dishes.

SASSAFRAS cleans you out. Try to find the root, better than the tea bags. The bigger the bark the better the tea. The best sassafras is to be found around Savannah, Georgia.

PARSLEY TEA is good for dropsy and promotes the menses.

MINT makes a delicious tea. A little mint mixed with orange pekoe makes an excellent iced drink.

RUE suppresses the menses. *Attention:* Use very sparingly. An overdose might drive you crazy.

SAGE is an excellent winter tea. Sage and honey are good for the liver, rheumatism and consumption.

BARK FROM PINE TREE is used to make tar water—a good spring clean out.

ROSEMARY is good for headaches. Mixed with borax, it's a healthy hair wash which is said to prevent baldness.

MARJORAM as a tea promotes the menses. In cooking, it's good for flavoring.

FENNEL is said to have an aphrodisiacal nature. But don't quote me. I just heard it through the grapevine. Fennel tea is said to also stop the hiccups and keeps you slim.

CUMIN It's an ancient Egyptian belief that cumin tea keeps your husband home. It is said that Cleopatra used it on Antony.

White Folks and Fried Chicken

White folks act like they would starve for sure if they couldn't have a hunk of meat. Eating neck bones don't bother me.

NECK BONES

PORK Stew down with Irish potatoes and fresh string beans or use as the boiled meat in greens.

LAMB Cook same as pork. Sometimes I cook lamb neck bones with coconut cream, carrots and fresh garden peas.

BEEF I use beef neck bones for everything that you would use pork neck bones. Try cooking black-eyed peas with beef neck bones instead of ham hocks.

TURKEY NECKS AND FRESH NECK BONES are delicious stewed down with barbecue sauce, tomato sauce and Ac'cent. Cook until tender.

White folks be talkin' about classic and they mean Beethoven (he was supposed to be a brother, anyhow) and French cook-

ing. Classic to me is James Brown and soul food. If you check
out the difference between what black and white folks eat it
ain't no wonder they can't get along. French folks always cov-
ering up the meat with some sauce or another. Most of the time,
it is to cover up the rancid taste of the meat. Poor as we
was, we never ate no bad meat. My mother would take it
back or throw it away before she cooked it for us. Black folks
spend more money for food than white folks. White folks can
take a can of tuna fish and feed multitudes. If we couldn't
have meat we had greens and rice and we ate plenty of that
but my mother never cooked none of that weird "tuna casserole." We never ate cold-storage chickens either. My grandmother still don't.

We used to go soon every Sunday morning to the poultry
market on Ridge Avenue (it was an ex-Jewish neighborhood
so stores were open on Sunday) and get our chickens. When
I was old enough, my mother let me go by myself and I'd
stick my hand in the cage and squeeze the breast of the
chicken, like I'd seen my mother do. I'd reject several (she
said don't take the first one that the man tries to push off on
you) and when my mother would say that I'd picked a good
one, I'd feel very proud of myself. The man would give us
chicken feet for free or maybe twelve for ten cents, depending
on how big a chicken we got.

CHICKEN FEET STEW

Cover chicken feet with boiling water. Grab the skin in the
middle of the gristle and pull it off. It should come off in one
piece. Cut the nails and put the feet in a pot and bring to
a boil. Simmer with plenty of onions and bell pepper until
tender. Delicious on grits, rice, hoecakes or anything else you
want to eat it on.

The best fried chicken I ever had was at my Cousin Haygood Smart's house at Bo Peep Crossing in Fairfax.

I hadn't seen them in five years. I arrived one evening just
about sunset. We drove up in the yard and I hid in the back
seat of the car. Uncle Bubba told Haygood that he had a pack-
age for him that came all the way from New York City. He
said to come out to the car and get it off the back seat. As
Haygood came to the car, up I popped. Haygood screamed,
"Cout is here," and all the Smarts came running. "Cout" was
my nickname that the Smarts called me. "Doll" is what the
Ritters call me. (Because I was so tiny, my mother carried
me around in a pillow till I was a year old.) The instant love
made me cry. We all hugged and kissed and they grabbed the
children (whom they had never seen) and smothered them
with hugs and kisses, too.

Aunt Carrie said, "Child, I know you're hungry," and she
told the children to pick up some sticks for the fire. She made
a fire in the stove, got some water from the well, put the
kettle on the fire to boil. Then she grabbed the first chicken
she could catch and wrung his neck. In a minute the chicken
was withering on the ground and his head in Aunt Carrie's
hand. By this time, the water was ready. She put the chicken
in a pan, poured the boiling water over him, plucked him,
cleaned him, singed him, and fried him. While he was frying,
she put the grits on and opened a jar of tomatoes that she had
put up last year and fixed them. Directly we had grits, fried
chicken, stewed tomatoes and biscuits by lamplight.

People up here act like it's going to a lot of trouble just to
give you a glass of water and whenever those vibrations hit
me, I remember how Aunt Carrie with no electricity, no run-

ning water, no gas, no refrigerator, not even an icebox got us a beautiful supper with love. I know that northern folks are out to lunch and better go down south and get their soul card punched. Mark Twain once said "the women of the north cannot fry chicken."

I use all parts of the chicken. The chicken livers are delicious. I fry mine in butter and add very thinly sliced onions when they are almost done. Grits and chicken livers make a nice Sunday morn breakfast. Sometimes I make a chicken heart stew; other times I combine the hearts and gizzards and make a giblet ragout. Then again I sometimes fry the gizzards by themselves. Giblet ragout and brown rice and Mary Greenly's green salad makes a nice Saturday night supper.

I always buy a whole chicken because it is cheaper by the pound.

I was very surprised to find how few modern women know how to cut up a chicken. Some supermarkets only sell whole chickens.

Chicken wings are very good too. Fry or smother or barbecue just like you would for the whole chicken. Fold the wing tips back for easier frying. Chicken wings are not expensive. You can get three pounds for a dollar.

A friend of mine gave me a recipe for

REDNECK RAGOUT

Take 12 chicken necks and stew them down with salt and pepper and garlic. When they are done remove the meat from bone and put it back in pot. Add a No. 2 can tomato sauce. Serve on grits or light bread.

This dish costs 5¢ a serving and will serve from 3 to 5 people—depending on how much they dig rednecks.

Everyone has their own way of frying chicken.

Barbara Carter fries her chicken with a cover.

I do not.

Dorothy White has a special way of frying unfloured chicken with ginger.

My mother fries hers unfloured and when it is just about done adds onions and a little water. Fry for a few minutes longer with a tight cover.

Joe Overstreet gave me a delicious recipe.

CHICKEN OVERSTREET

Salt and pepper the cut up chicken. Shake in a paper bag in flour. Fry in oil until golden brown. Remove excess grease and add 1 bottle orange soda pop. Cover and smother for 15 minutes.

The poet Larry Neal is one of the oldest friends I got. I didn't mean that Larry is old, he is a fine fly young man. I mean I've known him longer than anybody except Sol Battle and Charlie Fuller. What I really mean is I've know people longer but when you grow up in neighborhoods like mine it's kind of unusual to have fifteen-year friends. I was talking recently to my cousin Junior and I asked him how everyone on the block was doing and he said, "They are doing time that's how they are doing. The rest are dead."

Larry is a Virgo like Ted and Marion. Virgos and Aries are not supposed to get along but since I ain't never read no astrology books by black people I'll keep on getting along with my Virgo friends. I don't see Larry much. Isn't it funny that you don't see the folks closest to you as much as you do the others? When I was living on First Street, Larry came by one afternoon and stayed for dinner. We hadn't seen each other for a long time and I was cooking a chicken for dinner. I took the chicken and soaked it for 3 hours so we could talk. The result is what I call

NEAL FRIED CHICKEN

Take a cut up chicken fryer and season it with salt and pepper. Put in a bowl and add a mixture of milk and beaten eggs. Soak for 3 hours, turning often. Then proceed with fried chicken recipe.

CHICKEN CARLENE POLITE

See page 155

The Jet Set and Beautiful People

Jet set parties are dull, they don't know how to party. Folks be walking around with a thousand dollars' worth of clothes and ain't spent but a few dollars on the food for the party. They just stand around and sip drinks and eat hors d'oeuvres and when they do dance, they have that weird dude Myers or Lanin—whatever his name is. Seems to me they would do better to get some Otis Redding and Aretha Franklin and Wilson Pickett records. Look like they could fry up a few chickens and make a bunch of potato salad and buy a couple gallons of wine and be into something but instead they just stand around and look foolish. That is another thing I don't understand, how come they look so foolish? I wouldn't pay no faggot six hundred dollars to dress me up like a fool. I was reading that in the paper about "the right people." Now REALLY. The "right people" look wrong to me.

My Aunt Florrie Mae has worked in the fields all her life, cooked all her own meals, borne and raised four children and she look like a princess. Only thing she sometimes use on her face is a touch of nut-brown powder. The "right people" got

maids and governesses and good food and all that and most of
the women's faces look like *le plan linge le metro,* and when
you read one of those dumb reports about their parties, they
say, "All the beautiful people were there." Lord give me
strength.

They always talking bout the beautiful people. The jet set
is jive. I know some of the most beautiful people in the world:
Like René cutting the fool, A.B. doing the Bugaloo, Richie
Havens singing "Follow," Stella Beck and her vibration, Lillian playing the guitar and Lee Otis digging Lillian playing the
guitar, Charles Lloyd playing the flute and dancing at the
same time, Bob Fletcher singing "Suzanne" on the Long Island
Expressway, Nina Simone laughing and Franco on the Appian
Way.

Lou Gossett walking. Peggy talking. Nandi and Chandra
dancing. Leroi Jones reading his poetry. Ella and her purple
wrap. Granchan Moncour III just standing still. And Estella
Smart driving her Cadillac down Norris Street. Sam and Dave
on Salita del Grillo, Don Cherry walking down Avenue B in
those sky-blue pants and Deacon Wilson on a Sunday morning.
Marc *à la coupole,* Donald Hubbard in his orange tunic,
Marion and Sun Ra and sunset in Montparnasse, Yvette's face,
Aunt Hattie making cakes, and that Oxonian-talking horn
player playing the blues.

And let me tell you about Millie. Miss Mildred Thompson.
From Jacksonville, Florida. Millie lives in Germany now. Millie
is a painter. She is one of the best we got. She's a Pisces like
Charles. Millie used to have a studio on Third Street right
by Second Avenue. We used to stop and see her all the time.
Some days she'd get real evil and put us out. She and Chandra
would get into it and we'd all leave cause we are a close
family and stick together. But when Millie and Chandra would
get along we would have a really good time. Millie would show
us her latest work and we would rap about art and the fact

that in a country that discriminates against color, sex and intelligence, a black intelligent woman catches hell. Millie had a hot plate and used to cook up all kinds of soul food. She could cook some good one-pot things on that hot plate. All kinds of different beans and rice and meats mixed up together. One thing she made that was out of sight was

PEAS AND RICE

First boil smoked neck bones in coconut water. Then cook any kind of peas in a large pot with enough liquid to cover. Add celery, green peppers, thyme, salt and pepper. Cover and bring to a boil. Simmer for about 2 hours, stirring frequently. After 2 hours, add the rice and cook for another 20 minutes. *Attention:* Make sure you have a little extra coconut water on hand—you may need to add it with the rice.

To make coconut water: Punch out one of the three eyes in the coconut and drain the coconut water. Grate the coconut meat and add 3 cups of cold water. Put it in a mixing bowl lined with cheese cloth and squeeze. Add it to the original coconut milk and you got it.

Note: You can buy coconut water or coconut milk (whatever you want to call it). If you can't find it in your neighborhood, try Bedford-Stuyvesant. They got plenty of West Indians there. Or else you can make it yourself if you can't get a taxi to take you to Brooklyn.

Make sure your coconut has water in it, because it once took me all day running around Rome to find coconuts. When I finally found them, the woman said they were a dollar a piece. So I shook it to see if it was real and she shook her head and said, *"Coconut, si, aqua, no."* I told her I never heard of a fresh coconut that didn't have any liquid. She said maybe where I come from they have liquid, but not in Italy.

So I bought dried coconut and made the above coconut milk, which I had to have to make kalalou for my party that night at the Marquis Durrazzo's palazzo in Rome. About thirty people were there. Most them were soul folks from home: Donald, Elenore, Peter Outlaw, Robert from Watts, Joannie from Savannah, Teddy and some very hip Romans. Franco, Mimo who dug the Senegalese chicken the most because he said it was a beautiful earth color and sexy-looking; Carlo, Paul Getty and his wife (she dripped black-eyed peas on her suede skirt and I said, "Try to get it off immediately because it's very expensive to have suede cleaned . . ."). She just smiled and said, "I think it'll be all right." I didn't know she was the daughter-in-law of the richest man in the world. Isabelle and Florence and Miriam were there. The menu was kind of international soul. Fried chicken (the chickens were Italian and kind of fat). Senegalese chicken made with fresh Italian tomatoes and imported peanut butter—peanut butter from the Congo. Black-eyed peas—I brought them from home. I never travel without a couple of bags of black-eyed peas in my suitcase. Kalalou or the nearest thing to it I could make. I used Russian crabs for the kalalou, frozen Mediterranean shrimp (the marquis is in the frozen fish business), Uncle Ben's rice—yeah, they sell that in Rome too, fried Italian mullet and Italian-grown mustard greens and mangoes and watermelon and champagne.

* * * *

Carlene Polite is something else. Lord, that's a beautiful woman. She reminds me of Billie Holiday. Emily and Carlene and Julia and I were on a panel, *Pour pouvoir noir.* They have a group called the "Friends of SNCC" and they raise hell in Paris to end oppression of colored folks there. Anyhow, they needed someone to read a LeRoi Jones poem in English— the poem from the *Evergreen Review* that Judge Knapp wanted to give him five years for writing. Nobody wanted to do it, so I said, "If he can write it, I can read it—I ain't scared." There I was next to Carlene reading "up against the wall." Meanwhile, I was three days late getting back home in New York City and Oscar was fed up with Kali and Chandra and threatened to get the International Police. The next day I finally got on the plane, I was kind of nervous. I didn't know if Oscar's International Police would get me for being late or the House Un-American Committee for reading the poem in a foreign country or the Customs for all the food I brought home! I told you all that I never travel without taking black-eyed peas from home. Well, I never come home without bring-ing food in my bags. This time I had a baggette under my right arm, a ripe Camembert, a plastic bag of dried Congolese gombo, six macabos, one kilo of atadjos, a drawing Franco gave me under the left arm, three earthenware pots, two jars of instant French coffee (just like TV), four packages of dried Vietnamese soup, three large cans of Crème de Marrons de l'Ardèche (the cans are so art nouveau), a half dozen tubes Moutarde Forte de Dijon, three tubes Teklac, one kilo Farine de Manioc, all that was in my purse and I was holding my orange and red jeweled silver-handled Italian umbrella in my hand. I had to put my passport and other papers in my teeth cause my hands was full up. The man asked me how long I had been out. I got mad because I thought he meant Bellevue, but he meant out of the country. Anyhow, Carlene is a real soul sister. When I read her book, *Les Flagellants,* I flipped. It's very together. In Paris, Emily took me to meet her and she was at once warm and friendly. She had had dinner, but saw we were hungry and gave us a delicious buffet.

CHICKEN CARLENE POLITE

In the morning take a chicken, cut him up, salt and pepper him. Fry 'im in *huile d'arachide* (peanut oil). Cool him in a warm oven for ½ hour. She served it with hot rolls and cold wine.

*   *   *   *

"SOCK IT TO ME, SISTER." I stopped and turned round and round to see who could have said that on the Via del Corso in Rome. And there was Peter Outlaw. I put out my hand and he hit it.

What are you doing here? You mean they let *you* back in! Child, where can you get some soul food around here? Ain't none, but I know a hip dude from Milan who got a joint and food ain't too bad. See you this evening and we'll go there. So we did. The food was good. First we had

OUTLAW SPAGHETTI

Boil spaghetti and rinse in a colander with lots of cold water. Drain well. While the spaghetti is cooking, in a skillet fry cloves of garlic and whole red peppers in olive oil just for a hot minute, not long enough for the garlic to burn. Add the spaghetti and salt and heat for another hot minute.

A friend of Peter's came with us and he was too much. He was talking about how beautiful Rome was, in the taxi, on the way to the restaurant. As he was looking out the window and really digging it, he turned and said, "Can you buy ruins?" He was a brother from the south and we talked about the southland how in the old days you had to drive straight through cause wasn't no hotels or motels for black folks. We were talking about cars and he said he had had his Rolls-Royce painted another color cause gray was too dull and that the only reason Rollses came in them dull colors was cause black folks and Puerto Ricans wasn't buying them. But they would have to lighten up cause things were changing.

Then we had

ROMAN SALTIMBOCCA

Take Italian (thin) veal cutlets and cook at simmer in beef broth until almost done. Then add slices of half-cooked bacon on top of each one. Mix tomatoes, thyme, Parmesan cheese, olive oil, rosemary, butter and cook into a sauce, and put the sauce over each cutlet. Then top with grated Swiss cheese. Cook in oven for 15 minutes or until cheese melts.

SOME LETTERS TO
AND FROM STELLA
AND
ONE TO BOB
THOMPSON

A LETTER FROM STELLA
SOMEWHERE IN BOLIVIA

Dear Verta Mae:

Child I can't even pronounce the name of the town let alone write or spell it. So let's just say that I am in a small town in Bolivia. I am leaving in a few minutes. Matter of fact I am just writing to you while waiting to board my plane. I'm in the town where Regis Debray is in prison and it is very weird. People look at me like there was something hanging off me. They are all uptight about this Debray thing. Doesn't Debray look just like Oscar? I came thinking that I could get an interview but it was impossible. I'll write from Brazil.

Love,
Stella

P.S. This recipe is what I had for dinner last night. You can use it in your book but make sure you call it

PALTAS DEBRAY

Cut 3 round avocados in half. Fill with a salad made of diced chicken and shrimp and mayonnaise and hard-cooked egg mixed together. Sprinkle with lemon juice.

Stella,

Monday mornings are the worst! Robert Kennedy said in 40 years (that was a few years ago so we ain't got to wait that long) a black man can become president. I sure hope I can hang on until then. I hope the first thing that "our" President does is exempt all black folks from work, school, business, etc. on Monday mornings. Black folks won't have to do nothing until Monday afternoon. No matter how hard I try on Sunday to get ready—Monday mornings are always untogether.

I'm saying all this to say that I'll be writing you later in the week when I'm more together.

Love—
V. Mae

P.S. Here's the beer beef dish you wanted.

BEER BEEF

Use a Dutch oven and brown the stew beef in oil and butter mixture. When just about brown add chopped onions, minced garlic, crushed thyme, salt and pepper. Sauté all together for a few minutes longer, then add a couple cans of beer (enough to cover). Bring to a boil and cook on simmer until meat is tender, adding beer as needed.

Verta Mae,

You ain't seen nothing until you see Brazil. Everybody got some colored blood. They drink the hell out of coffee here. And eat some black beans. Girl I thought about that record you got by Archie, "The Girl from Ipanema." You should see the girls on that beach, they are some fine sisters. I went down there and felt like Cleopatra must have felt when Liz Taylor got her role in the movie. The sisters have got it. I am learning all kinds of dance steps. Tell Chandra I will teach them to her when I get back. My love to you all. Take care of yourself and try not to worry too much. I don't think Nixon will really be elected.

Love,
Stella

Stella,

Remember that lady who lived on F.D.R. Drive that we met in the Club 17? I saw her yesterday and she said she is going home! She said she was fed up with New York. She had had a bit of trouble with her son and she was depressed and lonely. She tried to talk to her neighbors but said it seemed like people up here don't want to be bothered with other people's problems. She said, "I'd rather go home and tie 'bacco and be with my people than live in this cold ass town." She is leaving Saturday.

Had a nice dinner party last night. John Chandler fixed candles in the tole chandelier and I put the fancy lace tablecloth on the table and we ate: palm heart and water cress salad, Neal fried chicken, coconut sweet potatoes, kalalou, avocados, mangoes, brown rice and several different types of wine. I thought that people who ate potatoes wouldn't take the rice, or if they had kalalou they wouldn't have the chicken. Well child, they took some of everything. I said, "You all ain't supposed to do that! If you eat the potato you don't have to eat the rice too." I told them that is how cultured white folks do. The hostess provides a selection and you make a choice. They said that they didn't know. They thought that they was supposed to eat all that I put out and not to partake of everything would be bad manners.

I guess it's a cultural gap.

We had a good time. They came over about seven and stayed until 2 A.M. John went out to lunch, but he came back so it was all right. Barbara couldn't come because the baby sitter had a nervous breakdown, so she stayed home to take care of Malik. David came, but later. Jacques and Ann Jones came and brought me some sassafras that Ann's mother brought back from Georgia. Nancy Chandler, Marc, Barbara and even R.N. came—but he didn't dance.

Child, I got to go, my sweet potato pie is burning.

Love
V.M.

Stella,

Girl, I had to send for my mother. The children had me up against the wall of motherhood. Things are a little bit better now, but my mother leaves tomorrow.

As far as the astrology thing goes, lots of folks don't think it is valid but I do. I know there is something to it. After all, Lou and Gyland and Bob and Oscar and René and Archie and Che are Geminis and Martin Luther King was a Capricorn and Hitler was an Aries.

This is the short'nin bread recipe you asked for.

Love—
V. Mae

SHORT'NIN BREAD

Take 3 cups flour and mix with 1 cup brown sugar and add ½ pound butter.

Lay it out on a floured board (or between two sheets of wax paper) and flatten it out and cut into squares. Bake for 20 minutes.

London

Verta,

Just found a terrific super super groovy apt. Girl, it is just as difficult to find an apt. here as there. Folks don't want to rent to colored and when they do, what they want you to live in is worse than that apt. I used to have on Norfolk St. I just couldn't take it. I asked a white girl I know to front for me and then I sublet from her. The apt. is not that good but it is decent. Some of my friends are giving me static. They say that I have gone middle class.

Love,
Stella

Stella dear,

Don't worry about being called middle class. Child, just go on and do what you got to do. What's so middle class about wanting enough to eat and a decent place to live? I am sick of the roaches and mice. I'm tired of cleaning the dirt off the floors so that when the children walk barefoot and get into bed the sheets won't get dirty cause when you go to the laundry and have dingy sheets white folks look at you like you was born nasty.

I'm tired of not having a decent bathroom.
I'm tired of being poor.
I'm tired of being tired.
I'm tired of walking these maggoted streets.

If decent living is middle class, then they can sock me some from the middle.

Love,
Verta

Verta,

I gave my first dinner party in the new place. I cooked for days and days. You are right about the cultural gap in cooking. My neighbors complained about the strange smells coming out of my apt. I was so mad. I think I might cook some chitlins all day long just to really give them a good smell. They so used to eating smelless and tasteless food that they get uptight if you fry an onion. They keep stiff upper lips and are very well mannered. Nothing smells. It would be bad manners. Anyhow girl, I played my Sam and Dave records and we danced and ate and didn't pay them no mind.

Here are the things I made last night. I'm getting to be almost as good a cook as you and Dorothy.

Stella

Stella,

I know what you mean by those well mannered types. I wouldn't let none of them come in to eat if I was you. Good manners ain't nothing but acting in a natural considerate manner towards others. But they make manners seem unnatural. If I cook a dinner for you with your consideration in mind how natural is it for you to sit there and eat and wait until the dinner is over before you say a word about the food. Wonder how well mannered people make love?

Verta Mae

Dear Verta,

Everybody getting upset over the black nationalists. They ain't seen nationalists till they check these French out. Ain't

nothing nothing if it ain't French (they a bitch with their shit).
French wine, French perfume, French food, French clothes,
French cigarettes, French beaches, French women, French sex,
French ice cream. Well, they got it. I'm getting the hell out of
here. *Haute cuisine* and *haute couture* is a bunch of *haute
merde.*

Stella

P.S. Forgot to mention that they don't even like each other.
Child, it is not enough just to speak French, you must have a
Parisian accent. Some dude spent an hour explaining to me the
difference in the way that people from 16 eme spoke and the
people who live in 5 eme. And yet when it all goes down they
will all gather together, sing the "Marseillaise" and die for the
glory of La France. Lift Every Voice and Sing. . . .

Stella

Stella,

You better be careful in Paris. Because the first evening I
was in Paris in '59, I met some people who would have sold
me into white slavery. Now dig that. Anyhow I was walking
down the Blvd. St. Michel and I was stepping, thinking to myself, Lord, is this really me in Paris France? Nineteen years
old and on my own. I made a vow to experience everything
that came my way. I wanted to live the bohemian life and I
wasn't scared of nothing cause life was on my side. I didn't
know one word of French but who needs a language when
one lived life like I did. Right by the Café Dupont a brother
from Senegal came to me and said, "My sister my sister," and
I said *oui.* He invited me to have coffee in the café with
him and his friends. I said, "Oh how wonderful." I couldn't
believe my luck. In Paris for only two hours and I had a gang
already. We had coffee and after a while they asked if I wanted

to go to an African night club. "Oh how wonderful," said I and off we went.

The owner was a friend of "my new gang." He asked me what do you do and I said, "Ah ah ah CHANTEUSE," so he announced to the whole club that Mlle. Kasmin (that's the name I used) from Harlem (in Europe people always say that black people are from Harlem or Mississippi) will chant for us Negro spirituals. I was shocked but I had made my vow so I sang "Swing Low, Sweet Chariot." They loved it and said, "Encore, encore." For an encore I did "Go Down, Moses." The owner said, "You're great. You've got the job." I said, "Job? What job?" He said yes come back every night and sing a song or two and we will pay you 2500 francs a night. 25NF=$5.00. Lord have mercy! This was more than I hoped for. Why I might be the next Jo Baker. So every night I would come to sing. But he would say, "Here are your francs you no sing tonight." It was getting kind of weird even for my "bohemian life." Finally one night he said that the band was going to Beirut and wanted me to go with them. I was excited. Thank you Jesus, I was going to see the world. By then I had another gang that I was hanging with and they was mostly painters. The whole beaux arts crowd. I hated to leave them but I said I had to go. Only reason that I didn't go to Beirut was cause the marines landed in Lebanon and Americans couldn't go there.

White slavery I found out is all them girls that come up missing every day in Paris. Mostly Nordic types but they get premiums for Nubians. I was a nineteen-year-old six-feet-tall Nubian virgin. Eight months later I read about the arrest of the club owner as one of the main white slavery men.

For one year I'd never walk by the Café Dupont. One day I walked by, I figured the crowd had changed by then, but there was François yelling "Kasmin—Kasmin—give me five— give me five." I ran like hell.

Verta

A LETTER FROM ROME FROM STELLA

Verta you were right! This is a decadent city. Makes *la dolce vita* look like one of them Doris Day Rock Hudson flicks. Child, what did you do here cause I went to the hotel that you told me to go to and when I told the woman I was your friend, she said they were filled up. Anyway it didn't matter because I ran into your friend Sliky and he found a place for me. The Harlem Globetrotters were staying there too. Hotel full of soul brothers. These Italian men are outside. They be screaming and pinching women on the street. One went to pinch me and I said, "Pinch me you guinea and I'll cut you." Dude kept on walking. Sliky is funny. He says that Europeans are primitive. Sliky says that the cross was used to teach them how to walk on twos and get up off fours. Ran into your friend Paolo and he had me over for lunch. I am sending you the recipe for the delicious pasta that he made. Hannibal must have put a real hurting on these people they got a thing about the Moors. Funny thing is that the further south you go the darker they get. The Moors must've gotten to some of their mamas. Look out Whitey, Black Power is gonna get your mamma.

Take care of the children and yourself,

Love, Stella

P.S. Saw Brock Peters and Dee Dee.

Stella,

Your letter was a day saver. The most horrible thing happened in fun city. They got rats on Park Avenue! But don't worry, Mayor Lindsay is on the case and promises to get rid of them. Probably drive them back to Harlem. Speaking of the mayor, was it in the paper there how during the fuel strike, when half of fun city was freezing, they got a picture of him at the airport headed for one of the Caribbean islands? Here is a recipe for a dish that I made last night.

Love,
Vert

KIDNEYS AND MUSHROOMS

Take thinly sliced lamb kidneys and sauté in peanut oil for 5 minutes. Add onions and sauté for 3 more minutes. Add mushrooms and parsley, salt, pepper and a bit of lemon juice. Simmer for 10 minutes.

Stella,

Sorry I haven't written. I was at the black power conference in Philadelphia. Will write all details later. Dig this . . . I was in a workshop and who walks in but cousin Rosemarie. With an afro. Dig this . . . who cut Rosemarie's afro? My cousin Maria. Maria has been blind since birth you know. And to top it off, at lunch time everyone was talking about the soul food truck outside selling fried chicken and greens. And guess who was running the truck? Guess who has five soul food trucks all over the city? My cousin, Rosemarie's father, Walter Ritter! Will write report on black power conference next time.

Love,
Verta Mae

Dear Vert,

Everything is everything.
I have a house and a job and third world boy friend. His
father is Vietnamese and his mother is African.
Please send some Sam and Dave records.

Love,
Stella

Girl,

Go head on with yo bad self.
I will be sending the records next week. Right now I am
broke. But wait, as soon as I am rich and famous I'm going
to change up. This is my wish list.

1. Move into a hotel for the winter.

2. Hire José Feliciano to sing to me in Spanish every morning
that I cook grits and fry fish.

3. Buy all new underwear from Sweden.

4. Go see Johnnie Mae in Aspen for the weekend.

5. Buy seventeen gold bangles for my left arm and four
silver rings for my right hand.

6. Give Uncle Bubba $1000 cash and get indoor plumbing
put in for him.

7. Give Kali a first edition of Langston Hughes.

8. Get a maid to wash the bathtub.

9. Have the *Amsterdam News* delivered every Thursday
noon.

10. Have a dozen persimmons and scrambled eggs and five bottles of Brillante rosé wine for Sunday morning breakfast.

11. Send for my mother.

And that ain't all, I want to see beauty and hear truth. That's just how bad I am.

                              Love,
                              Sister V. Mae

Dear Verta,

Girl, those people you told me to look up were out to lunch. From now on I will not ask you for any more addresses. They are your *friends*. You all got it . . . together. I'm going to pray for you. What did you mean by that "food is life?"

                              Stella

Stella,

You want to know why I say soul food is life? Well, first off, food ain't nothing but food. No matter who you are and where you live you got to eat. Cooking is a creative thing. Cooking is one of the highest of all the arts. It can make or break life. The world must be Gemini cause more manure has hit the fan over the twins' love and hunger than any other forces. So, if you cook with love and feed people, you got two forces cooled out already. Dig, food can cause happiness or unhappiness, health or sickness and make or break marriages.

I read the other day where this cat said that a lot of interracial marriages break up because of the cultural gap in cooking. Remember when you know who used to serve cottage cheese and frozen fish to you know who? Remember he used to come over to your house and cook pork chops?

Anyhow, soul food depends on what you put in it. I don't mean spices either.

If you have a serious, loving, creative energetic attitude towards life, when you cook, you cook with the same attitude.

Food changes into blood, blood into cells, cells change into energy which changes up into life and since your life style is imaginative, creative, loving, energetic, serious, food is life. You dig.

Vert

Verta,

Thanks for the letter food is life. I broke up with my old man. I really feel bad. My heart beats heavy every time somebody even mentions his name. If your food is life stuff is true then I ain't got no life. I ain't got nobody to cook for.

Stella

Stella,

Get a holt of yourself. Spring is coming and there will be new songs to sing.

Love,
Verta Mae

P.S. Thanks to Dr. Christiaan Barnard, we now know that the heart that beats for you is not always your own.

Dear Verta,

Did you read *The Confessions of Nat Turner* by William Styron? Girl, it is another example of nothing.

Ossie Davis is correct. He says, "I find this book to be

false to black history and an insult by implication to black womanhood. Styron's implications about black men and black rebellion is that what agitates the black man is not a search for freedom, but a search for white women!"

I did a bunch of reading on Nat Turner and that man (Styron) has told a big lie. A flagrant low-down dirty lie against one of our heroes.

You will be interested to know that for Nat's last meal he had roast pork and apple brandy.

I didn't have an oven so I made an apple pork thing on top of the stove. It's enclosed and I will close. Ha.

Stella

NAT TURNER APPLE PORK THING

Salt the bottom of the skillet and fry seasoned pork steaks. When brown on both sides add peanut oil and cook until done. Add thinly sliced onions and quartered apples and cook for 15 minutes in covered skillet.

Dear Verta Mae,

Child, you would not believe this. This is a beautiful country. The people are very soulful. They look like Puerto Ricans with towels. Only thing they don't eat no pork here. Girl, last night I went to a boss party. It was in a palace. Well, maybe the place wasn't really no palace but it beats Norfolk Street. I went and I was dressed to kill. You know that light blue dress you made for me? Well I wore the pink one that is something like it. These people know how to party. They had at least 85 courses. We sat on cushions and ate off a long low table. We ate with our hands and they had maids going

around with silver jugs of orange flower water to rinse our
fingers. Child, you should have seen me. I was in my act. The
food was in the middle of the table and you just dig in and
work out. It was out of sight. I am sending you a few
recipes for you to try out. The soil here is different so everything will taste different but it will be similar. They don't
use no chemical spray on their vegetables. I wish I had some
pictures took because I know that you will think that I am
lying. Kiss the children for me and give my love to everyone
at Pee Wee's. I'll be heading down to black Africa soon but
you can write me here at American Express.

Love,
Stella

MOROCCO LAMB STEW WITH PRUNES

Soak prunes overnight. Use the neck bones of mutton. Flour
and salt and pepper the meat and brown in butter in skillet.
Add chopped onions and brown. Now add hot water to cover.
Now add cinnamon, saffron and garlic and cook for 1½ hours.
Add the prunes and orange flower water and a bit of sugar.
Let cook for 1 hour more.

BAMYA
from Egypt

In an iron skillet sauté 1 pound cubed lamb. When lamb is
just about brown add diced garlic, salt and pepper, diced
tomatoes and gombos.

Sauté in the skillet for a few minutes and then remove to
a saucepan and add 2 cups water and cook for 1 hour.

Dear Verta,

I have said it before but this time I mean it. Don't send me no more names and addresses. I am not interested in looking up any more of your friends. With friends like you got you don't need enemies. I have started eating in more than ever now. I try to use all the spices and have developed a penchant for cumin. Here's my recipe.

Love,
Stella

EL COMINO REAL

Season (salt, pepper, garlic) a cut up chicken and marinate in a little lemon juice and peanut oil and onions for 1 hour. Then add cumin powder, tomatoes, zucchini and cook for ½ hour.

Dear Stella,

Stop talking about my friends. I know they are crazy. But to tell it like it is, any nigger who ain't crazy in this society is out of his mind.

Verta Mae

P.S. Get the January 24 issue of *Time* magazine. Look under food.

I had to write them a letter. Enclosed is a copy.

VM

January 24th

SIRS:

You have the bad taste to say that soul food is tasteless. Your taste buds are so racist that they can't even deal with black food. Your comment that the "soul food fad" is going to be short-lived is dumb. But then your whole culture is made of short-lived fads. So you white folks just keep on eating that white foam rubber bread that sticks to the roof of your mouth, and keep on eating Minute Rice and instant potatoes, instant cereals and drinking instant milk and stick to your instant culture. And I will stick to the short-lived fad that brought my ancestors through four hundred years of oppression. *Time* magazine couldn't take any more and stopped here. Collard greens are thousands of years old and in the days of the Roman Empire were considered an epicurean delight. French restaurants too widely renowned even to depend on stars given by Guide Michelin serve chitlins sausages, only they call it *andouillette*. Soul food is more than chitlins and collard greens, ham hocks and black-eyed peas. Soul food is about a people who have a lot of heart and soul. Ask Doctor Christiaan Barnard about them black hearts.

Verta Mae

Verta Mae,

Child, after 350 years, I am home. Africa, the motherland. You better pack up your children and come on over. It is not true that the Africans don't like or want us. Biggest lie the white man ever told. He told the Africans that we didn't like them either. Divide and conquer is his game but it is over. The brothers and sisters are coming home. There are so many things to do and see. And girl, the Europeans have robbed these countries blind of their art. Rockefeller ought to get up off his million dollar primitive art collection and give it back. The English are said to have melted down some of the Benin sculpture during World War II to make bullets. I wouldn't put it past them. The markets are the best. I go two times a day. Everyone looks familiar. I saw a dude here on the street looked just like Kelly. Child, you would flip over the markets. They got greens that they ain't even got names for. I'm sending you a bunch of recipes. How come Dorothy and White moved to Brooklyn? Is Rap Brown out of jail? I sent SNCC $500. Give the children my love and kiss them for me. I'll write again when I get my nerves together. This place has blown my mind. I am never going to leave. I'm only sorry that I'm going to miss Jessie's wedding.

Love,
Stella

LUMUMBA GOMBO
from Kinshasa

Salt and pepper the cut up chicken and brown in peanut oil. When it is golden brown add chopped onions and diced garlic and brown the onions. Then add tomatoes and gombos and cook for 45 minutes and add spinach. Cover and cook for 10 minutes more.

BOEUF AUX GOMBOS
from Cameroons

In a skillet brown 1½ pounds of salted and peppered and floured beef chunks. Then add chopped onions and diced garlic. Remove to a covered saucepan and cook until tender.

Then thicken sauce with paste of water and manioc flour. Add hot pepper, tomatoes and sliced gombos and cook for another ½ hour.

NORTHERN LABAJABAJA

(an adaptation of a Senegalese dish)

Use your biggest blackest skillet and take a cut up chicken and brown in butter-peanut oil mixture. After the chicken is brown, add chopped up onions and chopped bell peppers. Brown for a minute. Then add chicken broth. Remove to a deep casserole and add coconut cream and sweet potatoes. Cook until chicken is done. Then add raw spinach for 5 more minutes.

Stella,

I heard O. C. Smith on the radio singing, "If God didn't make little green apples" and it made me wonder about God. Does he give a damn? I thought about those immoral heart transplants. Who is to say who can have whose heart? Does God give you life or does Dr. Barnard? I'll bet Dr. Barnard don't sleep none too tough at night. Bet you he has to take Cope and Excedrin and aspirin and Bufferin and native brew before he goes to bed. Even so, I bet the haint rides him every night. That is some weird stuff he pulled. First he puts poor Clive's heart in the body of a white man. Then he put the heart of a young pregnant black woman in the body of an old white ex-cop in Johannesburg, South Africa. God don't love ugly? Do you, God?

Tell me, God, how could you let this happen? Was it because Clive was a coloured? What is a coloured? Is that

like being half pregnant? I got two children and I know there
ain't no such thing. Either you is or you ain't. Come on,
God. Give a damn. Right, Stella?

Verta Mae

Stella,

This morning we had no heat so I had to knock on the oven
door to let the mice know I wanted to use the oven. Went out
to buy some milk and a big fat brown rat crossed my path.
Picked up *Sex and the Single Girl* and read that when you
look for a job not to wear too much jewelry or you will look
like a Ubangi. Read the newspaper and saw that for Halloween
Dickie tricked and treated Liz to a big carrot ring, *Yellowback
Radio Broke Down* and a pig arrested a cake. Child, this
place is going to the dogs. On the other hand they say that
every dog has his day and good dogs have two.

V. Mae

P.S. I wrote the following note to H. G. Brown.

Dear Miss Brown,
You are white and right. I am a Ubangi.

Miss Smart

Bob Thompson,

I remember you. I went to your "memorial service" at the
Judson Church.
It was abstract.
Your mother and all her sisters were there waiting for them
to get into it.
Waiting for them to get into what you were about.

Waiting for them to get into the rhythm of your life style.

Waiting for them to feel.

But they didn't.

They just hemmed and hawed and talked and a singer sang.

A.B. stood up and recited a poem for you called "Didn't He Ramble." That was the only time I saw your mama and her sisters take out their freshly starched and ironed hankies.

I heard your mama say in response to A.B.'s "Didn't He Ramble"—"Oh yes, he did."

Oh yes, you did so go head on Bob and ramble.

If only that super liberal had been able to touch on something that struck the heart. I would have cried rivers for you.

After I left I told all my friends, "Please don't let them get holt of me if I die up here."

Don't let them have no "memorial service" for me.

Don't cremate me either.

Bury me next to my daddy and my brother and my grandfather and Aunt Virter and Uncle Howard.

Don't let them touch me.

Have a party—with Wilson Pickett and Otis Redding records.

Ask Miriam to sing "When I've Passed On," and Aretha to sing "Don't Let Me Lose This Dream."

And ask Nina to sing anything she feels.

Have lots of food.

Get Barbara Carter to make the barbecue chicken wings and Dorothy to make some potato salad.

Also let there be fried fish and turnip and mustard greens mixed together—smothered onions, home fries with pickapepper sauce and plenty wine and beer and plenty tangerine juice.

Be sure to tell Joanie so she can make the same palm heart and water cress salad she made for Marion.

Ask Lillian to make somethin' and my grandmother to make me a sweeten bread.

I don't even care if the whole affair is catered . . . just don't let them abstract folks have no service for me.

The last time I saw you, you had a split in the seam of your pants. We were on our way with Big Ray to see a show at the Guggenheim Museum. While I was getting ready, I offered some sweet potato pie to you and Ray. We never got to the show. The corn likker just knocked us out. We drank the whole thing and I was mad. I had gone to a lot of trouble to bring it here from South Carolina by train. On that train the rubber ring came off the Mason jar and it was dripping all over our shoe box lunch. The smell was very strong. Everyone kept looking at me and nobody would sit next to us. That was good cause it meant that we had the whole four seats to ourselves.

But I was very worried that I could be arrested.

I saw the headlines—MOTHER OF 2 ARRESTED TRANSPORTING BOOTLEG LIKKER THRU 5 STATES. And after finally getting it home—in one half an afternoon—you and Big Ray wiped it out. I was really mad, but now it don't matter much.

Verta Mae

TO BE CONTINUED

The Kitchen

THE KITCHEN IS THE MOST IMPORTANT ROOM IN MY HOME. TIS THE PLACE FROM WHICH I DO MY THING.

I EAT IN THE KITCHEN.

WHEN FRIENDS DROP IN SOMETIMES WE NEVER LEAVE THE KITCHEN.

I JUST DO EVERYTHING IN THE KITCHEN.

I WROTE THIS BOOK IN THE KITCHEN.

WHEN I SEW I SET UP THE SEWING MACHINE IN THE KITCHEN.

I IRON IN THE KITCHEN.

THE OTHER DAY I TRIED TO MOVE THE PIANO IN BUT COULDN'T GET ANYONE TO HELP ME.

THE CHILDREN DO THEIR HOMEWORK IN THE KITCHEN.

SOMETIMES THERE IS SO MUCH HAPPENING IN THE KITCHEN THAT I CAN'T GET TO THE STOVE TO COOK AND WE HAVE TO CALL CHICKEN DELIGHT.

A Poem

en la casa de verta

for on monday in 1969 on the streets
was diamonds. downtown society bodegas one
right after the other. avocado & tomato juice
spaceships parked in front of vertas house/sparkling
yellow metal with stickers from Venus Airlines
Moon Shuttle Jupiter Car Service Mars heliport
& all on monday by a bridge. 1969 year of the rooster
hot sauce/street beans . . . . . .
                            caribbean rice on the fire
with african beans warming
                      whow
                            the centuries & centuries
of sea exploration & mixing.
                      but here we all are
in vertas soul space kitchen
                      taking off.

                                    Victor Hernandez Cruz
                                    1969

Appendix 1

Introduction to the 1986 Edition

When I wrote *Vibration Cooking* seventeen years ago I had no idea it would be published. I wrote it because I wanted to do something creative. My daughters were young and I couldn't afford to take a class in anything nor pay a sitter. My creative activity would have to be done in the house. Writing seemed like the perfect thing. I wasn't a writer but people said they enjoyed my letters and besides, I was not writing to be published. I was writing to express myself. I loved to cook, had great food memories and experiences with friends and family in various places, so why not write about that. Put everything down and on special occasions give a copy of "writings" to the people I talked about. That's what I had in mind and that's what I did. I borrowed a typewriter from my next door neighbor and changed my life.

There is nothing like having a book published to change your life. Because of *Vibration Cooking* I did things, met people, and went places I had only dreamt about. And a few I had never dreamt of.

I was on the cover of *JET* magazine. I went to a barbecued chicken lawn party at the White House, a sit-down dinner at 21, and a picnic in the Bahamas. I talked about cooking on TV with "The

Galloping Gourmet" and cut up collard greens, fried chicken, and ate watermelon with Barbara Walters on "Not For Women Only." My daughter had a hamburger on "The Dick Cavett Show," I had a feijoada in Brazil on a Saturday, and a "Cuba Libre" in Havana. I catered a celebration for James Baldwin, Dr. Alvin Poussaint's wedding, a record party for David Bowie and the book party for *Vibration Cooking*.

Writing about people in a cookbook is like being rich. It's hard to know if they like you for *YOU* or what.

People get weird on you. They will stand in your face and say anything. "Hey, I'm go write me a cookbook! I can burn too!" "So, what qualifies you to write a cookbook?" Somebody actually asked one of my children if I could really cook. My daughter said "My mama cook like Aretha Franklin sing!" and that was that.

Once I overheard a friend asking someone if they had read *Vibration Cooking*. I was so happy. It was great to have your friends promoting your book. Well, I was happy until I heard "I'll send you a Xerox of page 45, that's the page I'm on. . . ."

I've been invited to dinner and then asked if I was going to put the host and the recipes in my next book. The answer is NO. *Vibration Cooking, #2* will be fiction. Only the recipes will be real. I don't have the energy to go through "How come you wrote about so and so and didn't mention me, I was there" . . . or "I cook better than she does. . . ."

Everybody's mama's cousin wanted a free copy of *Vibration Cooking*. After all, wasn't I exploiting and getting rich off their family recipes?

Members of my family had attitudes. My mother felt that I had made "too much 'miration" over my grandmother, her mother-in-law. My grandmother felt I had not made enough. Uncles, aunts, and cousins added their three cents . . . and so it went. "No!" no more autobiographical cooking notes. Your kitchen secrets will be safe with me. As Toni Cade Bambara wrote in *Gorilla, My Love*, . . . "It's best to deal in straight-up fiction."

The white folks were on my case, too. What was *VIBRATION COOKING*? Was it cooking with a vibrator? Was a geechee girl like a geisha girl? Was I trying to be a black Alice B. Toklas? The only thing I have in common with Alice B. Toklas is that we lived on the same street in Paris. I lived at #17 and she at #27, on the Rue des Fleurs.

The question I was most often asked was why didn't I consider myself a "soul food" writer. Over and over I would try to explain my philosophy on the nonracial aspects of blackeyed peas, watermelon, and other so-called soul foods on TV, radio, and in lectures. It seemed to me while certain foods have been labeled "soul food" and associated with Afro-Americans, Afro-Americans could be associated with all foods.

I would explain that my kitchen was the world. Indeed, I experimented with all the cuisines of the world. Each month I chose a country, and for every meal that month I would prepare only dishes from that country.

My feeling was/is any Veau à la Flamande or Blinchishe's Tvorogom I prepared was as "soulful" as a pair of candied yams. I don't have culinary limitations because I'm "black." On the other hand, I choose to write about "Afro-American" cookery because I'm "black" and know the wonderful, fascinating culinary history there is. And because the Afro-American cook has been so underappreciated.

I exploit Afro-American dishes every chance I get . . . for instance, collard greens. A bowl of collard greens does for me what a bowl of chicken soup does for others.

I love to turn people on to the nutritional and psychological values of collard greens. Although once, I'm ashamed to say, I might have been directly responsible for turning someone against collards.

One day I was in line at the greengrocer. It was the morning of a very bad day for me. One child had a fever and the other had chills. I was on deadline, the typewriter was broken, the rent was overdue, it was raining, and the roof was leaking—you know the kind of day I'm talking about. On days like that I always make a mess of greens. Besides the curative properties, the ritual of fixing the greens—handling each green personally, folding leaf unto leaf, cutting them up, etc.—cools me out!

So there I was, in line, holding my collard greens. A white woman asked me, "How do you people fix those?"

Now, more than likely if I had not been in such a Purple Funk, I might have let the "you people" go by, but this particular morning I didn't. "Salad," I said.

"Salad?"

"Yeah, salad."

"But I was sure You People cooked them."

"No, never. . . . Salad."

"What kind of dressing?"

"Italian!"

A black woman overheard the exchange. She looked at me as if I had discredited the race. I have often wondered if that white woman went home and actually made a collard green salad with Italian dressing.

According to my mother, I did discredit the race when I cooked collard greens on TV. It was on the "Not For Women Only" Ethnic Week cooking series. I was the "soul food" chef, and I was in a dilemma.

I wanted to use the opportunity to prove that Afro-American cookery was more than chitlins and pigs' feet, and at the same time I wanted to acknowledge the traditional dishes.

I decided to go with a traditional "Soul Food" menu, but I'd prepare the dishes in a nontraditional way. For example, the collard greens: Instead of ham hocks, I would use a seasoning of peanut oil and bouillon cubes.

I figured that would take care of the Muslims and the vegetarians. I didn't even think about my mother. I had no idea of the embarrassment she would suffer.

It seems that some of her church sisters saw the show.

"Mrs. Smart's daughter was on coast-to-coast TV and cooked naked greens!"

"What did you say?"

"Umhuhm, yes she did!"

"Where you think she picked that up?"

"Maybe she was raised like that."

"Umhuh, uumm, umm-umm!"

"It's a shame before the living justice, 'naked' greens."

"My, my, my . . ."

My choice of watermelon as the dessert on the show was controversial. Host Barbara Walters said, "Frankly," if it was up to her . . . she would not have chosen watermelon. Marie Brown, my editor, brought the watermelon to the studio. On her way, she ran into another black editor, who was horrified. "I wouldn't carry a watermelon in the streets for no author on no TV show!"

Scores of people called me up after the show to say that I should have chosen a menu that elevated "soul food."

Although *Vibration Cooking* was out of print for over a decade, I was constantly receiving letters from people who had "just discovered" the book. Sometimes they'd tell me how a certain recipe turned out, who they made it for, or who they were planning to make it for. Some people wanted to get in touch with their old friend "so and so" on page 83. . . . A lot of people said their copies had been stolen; where could they get another? Sadly, I would have to say, "It's out of print."

I am very happy that *Vibration Cooking* is back, for obvious reasons, and because a book is a great way to make friends. Take it from me, an autographed copy of your book will take you far. I've sent copies of *Vibration Cooking* to everyone I thought I might want to know, from politicians to movie stars.

I'm glad for another reason: the more books about Afro-American cookery, the better.

When *Vibration Cooking* came out in 1970, there were fewer than ten published cookbooks by Afro-Americans. There are not many more than that today. That's a scandal.

Books like Helen Mendes' *African Heritage Cookbook*, *Spoonbread and Strawberry Wine*, *Princess Pamela's Soul Kitchen*, Edna Lewis's *Country Cooking*, *The Ebony Cookbook*, and *A Light Hand and Warm Heart*, are wonderful celebrations of Afro-American cookery, but there should be a hundred more books on the subject. Afro-American cookery is like jazz—a genuine art form that deserves serious scholarship and more than a little space on the bookshelves.

A few months ago, at National Public Radio, I received a postcard from an irate man in New England. He wrote, "Ten years ago, I burned or threw away a book you wrote because of the disgusting remark you made about the Gay Community. Are you going to update that or do we have to organize a radio boycott? . . ."

I couldn't remember what remark he was referring to, so for the first time in sixteen years, I read *Vibration Cooking*. It made me a little crazy.

There were people and incidents I hadn't thought of in fifteen years. Some things I had completely forgotten. Other things I'd just as soon forget.

In the chapter called "The Jet Set and the Beautiful People" I found what offended the postcard writer. I used the word "faggot." I should have said "homosexual." I apologize for that and for "Roy Wilkins Sauce" on page 100, but the rest stands. The book is honest. It's what it is, what it was, and I live with it.

When I announced that *Vibration Cooking* would be reissued, the Vibration Cookers started working on my nerves, again. My mother said, "Praise the Lord." . . . Now I could write more about her. My daughters wanted an update. "Please put in that we grew up." One is a great cook and one is a great specialty cook. Another person wanted me to take him out of the book and leave his recipe in. Somebody else wanted me to take her recipe out and leave her in. One person actually gave me an update; she now lives in Blah-blah, was divorced from What's-his-name and living with So-and-so.

I love it!!!

The update on some of my friends is public knowledge. Archie Shepp is still blowing. . . . Donald Hubbard is a well-known European shoe designer. . . . Cynthia Belgrave is the director of her own theater company. . . . Vinnie Burrows's one-woman show is an international showstopper. . . . Sun Ra is in orbit. . . . Bill Larkins is a West Palm Beach lawyer, Lou Gosset won an Academy Award, and Charles Fuller won a Pulitzer Prize. Hart Leroi Bibbs is taking pictures in Paris, where Millie Thompson sculpts.

I haven't spoken to Millie in years. We had a falling-out and I vowed *never* to put Mildred's name in my mouth again. We fell out because when she returned to the States, after fifteen years, she came to my house and took off the wall the painting she had made and GIVEN to me.

About a years later, a woman named Deborah Amos, from National Public Radio, called me. "Would you be interested in doing commentaries on NPR, 'All Things Considered'?" "Sure." . . . Well, to make a long story short, it turns out that Deborah was/is a good friend of Millie's, and she said Millie spoke highly of me. So over the years I would get and send regards to Millie via Deborah. Although I have not spoken to her since our row, my association with her friend Deborah and NPR has been so rewarding, I almost forgive her.

I'm too sad to say that some of my favorite people didn't live to see *Vibration Cooking* come back. My dear friends Larry Neal; Aunt Bea; Uncle Bubba; Yvonne's mother. Mrs. Rose Sullivan; my beloved grandmother—Mother-Dear and Orde Coombs.

In 1969, a handsome young man came up to me in Peewee's legendary Lower East Side bar and asked, "Do you know a little girl named Kali?" I flippantly replied, "Yeah, she's my room-mate." He said, "My name is Orde Coombs. I work at Doubleday, Kali's poetry manuscript and your cookbook notes came in; I recognized you from the photos. Doubleday is interested in do-ing both projects. Why don't you come in tomorrow and meet the editors. It's my last day but I'd like to introduce you to them before I leave."

The next day, my daughter Kali and I went to Doubleday, and as they say, the rest is history.

Kali was nine years old when Doubleday published *Poems by Kali*. I won't tell you how old I was—my aunt Zipporah says, "A woman who tells her age will tell anything." In *Vibration Cooking* I have told all I'm going to tell.

New York City
February, 1986

Appendix 2

Introduction to the 1992 Edition

The third coming of *Vibration Cooking or The Travel Notes of a Geechee Girl* took me by surprise. I feel like a woman who had a baby but didn't know she was pregnant.

I do consider the baby a blessing. In the twenty-two years since the book was originally published in hardcover by my original editor, present agent, and dear friend, Marie Brown, there hasn't been a year that, in or out of print, something good hasn't come my way because of *Vibration Cooking*.

First time around in its hardcover incarnation, *Vibration* got lots of attention because it was a "Black" cookbook. Second time around in its mass market edition it got attention because it come back and most people didn't even know it was there the first time.

This time in its fabulous One World edition I don't know what's going to happen. Who knows what the reviewers will have to say about a twenty-two-year-old book that you might say slipped through the cracks for more than two decades and lived.

That's the mysterious thing. *Vibration Cooking or The Travel Notes of a Geechee Girl* was kept alive without the critics. Oh, there were reviews, but it was not reviewed. Without sounding too full of myself, I will say that *Vibration Cooking* was a book that the people made. *Vibration Cooking* was never a *New York Times* bestseller, but it was widely read because people shared it. People tell me that they loaned it to so-and-so, who gave it to so-and-so to read, who took it to Ohio so his mother could see it. . . .

Ron Walker tells this story. A few months after *Vibration Cooking* was published for the first time, he was in a barber's shop in Harlem. A guy came in selling books. Somebody asked for *Vibration Cooking or The Travel Notes of a Geechee Girl*, and the guy says, "I'm outta them, everybody wants that book. Who is the bitch?"

Nowadays, it would be politically incorrect to buy a stolen item in a barber shop and even more serious not to admonish anyone who called a woman a bitch, but that's the way it *was*!

When I wrote *Vibration Cooking* in 1970 I had no idea it would be published. I wrote it because I wanted to do something creative. My daughters were young and I couldn't afford to take a class in anything or pay a sitter. My creative activity would have to be done in the house. Writing seemed like the perfect thing. I wasn't a writer but people said they enjoyed my letters and besides, I was not writing to be published. I was writing to express myself. I loved to cook, had great food memories and experiences with friends and family in various places, so why not write about that. Put everything down and on special occasions give a copy of "writings" to the people I talked about. That's what I had in mind and that's what I did. I borrowed a typewriter from my next-door neighbor and changed my life.

There is nothing like having a book published to change your life. Because of *Vibration Cooking* I did things, met people, and went places I had only dreamt about. And a few I had never dreamt of.

I was on the cover of *JET* magazine. I went to a barbecued-chicken lawn party at the White House, a sit-down dinner at "21," and a picnic in the Bahamas. I talked with Ed Bradley about cooking on TV with "The Galloping Gourmet" and cut up collard greens, fried chicken, and ate watermelon with Barbara Walters on "Not for Women Only." My daughter had a hamburger on "The Dick Cavett Show," I had a feijoada in Brazil on a Saturday, and a "Cuba Libre" in Havana. I catered a celebration for James Baldwin, Dr. Alvin Poussaint's wedding, a record party for David Bowie and the book party for *Vibration Cooking*.

Writing about people in a cookbook is like being rich. It's hard to know if they like you for *YOU* or what.

People get weird on you. They will stand in your face and say anything. "Hey, I'm go write me a cookbook! I can burn too!" "So, what qualifies you to write a cookbook?" Somebody actually asked one of my children if I could really cook. My daughter said, "My mama cook like Aretha Franklin sing!" and that was that.

Once I overheard a friend asking someone if they had read *Vibration Cooking*. I was so happy. It was great to have your friends promoting your book. Well, I was happy until I heard "I'll send you a Xerox of page 45, that's the page I'm on. . . ."

I've been invited to dinner and then asked if I was going to put the host and the recipes in my next book. The answer is NO. *Vibration Cooking, #2* will be fiction. Only the recipes will be real. I don't have the energy to go through "How come you wrote about so-and-so and didn't mention me, I was there" . . . or "I cook better than she does. . . ."

Everybody's mama's cousin wanted a free copy of *Vibration Cooking*. After all, wasn't I exploiting and getting rich off their family recipes?

Members of my family had attitudes. My mother felt that I had made "too much 'miration" over my grandmother, her mother-in-law. My grandmother felt I had not made enough. Uncles, aunts, and cousins added their three cents . . . and so it went. "No!" no more autobiographical cooking notes. Your kitchen secrets will be safe with me.

The white folks were on my case, too. What was *VIBRATION COOKING*? Was it cooking with a vibrator? Was a geechee girl like a geisha girl? Was I trying to be a black Alice B. Toklas? The only thing I have in common with Alice B. Toklas is that we lived on the same street in Paris. I lived at #17 and she at #27, on the Rue des Fleurs.

The question I was most often asked was why didn't I consider myself a "soul food" writer. Over and over I would try to explain my philosophy on the universal aspects of black-eyed peas, watermelon, and other so-called soul foods on TV, radio, and in lectures. It seemed to me while certain foods have been labeled "soul food" and associated with African Americans, African Americans could be associated with all foods.

I would explain that my kitchen was the world. Indeed, I experimented with all the cuisines of the world. Each month I chose a country, and for every meal that month I would prepare only dishes from that country.

My feeling was/is any Veau á la Flamande or Blinchishe's Tvorogom I prepared was as "soulful" as a pair of candied yams. I don't have culinary limitations because I'm "black." On the other hand, I choose to write about "African American" cookery because I'm "black" and know the wonderful, fascinating culinary history there is. And because the African American cook has been so underappreciated.

I exploit African American dishes every chance I get . . . for instance, collard greens. A bowl of collard greens does for me what a bowl of chicken soup does for others.

I love to turn people on to the nutritional and psychological values of collard greens. Although once, I'm ashamed to say, I might have been directly responsible for turning someone against collards.

One day I was in line at the greengrocer. It was the morning of a very bad day for me. One child had a fever and the other had chills. I was on deadline, the typewriter was broken, the rent was overdue, it was raining, and the roof was leaking—you know the kind of day I'm talking about. On days like that I always make a mess of greens. Besides the curative properties, the ritual of fixing the greens—handling each green personally, folding leaf unto leaf, cutting them up, etc.—cools me out!

So there I was, in line, holding my collard greens. A white woman asked me, "How do you people fix those?"

Now, more than likely if I had not been in such a Purple Funk, I might have let the "you people" go by, but this particular morning I didn't. "Salad," I said.

"Salad?"

"Yeah, salad."

"But I was sure You People cooked them."

"No, never. . . . Salad."

"What kind of dressing?"

"Italian!"

A black woman overheard the exchange. She looked at me as if I had discredited the race. I have often wondered if that white woman went home and actually made a collard green salad with Italian dressing.

In 1969, according to my mother, I did discredit the race when I cooked collard greens on TV. It was on the "Not For Women Only" Ethnic Week cooking series. I was the "soul food" chef, and I was in a dilemma.

I wanted to use the opportunity to prove that African-American cookery was more than chitlins and pigs' feet, and at the same time I wanted to acknowledge the traditional dishes.

I decided to go with a traditional "Soul Food" menu, but I'd prepare the dishes in a nontraditional way. For example, the collard greens: Instead of ham hocks, I would use a seasoning of peanut oil and bouillon cubes.

I figured that would take care of the Muslims and the vegetarians. I didn't even think about my mother. I had no idea of the embarrassment she would suffer.

It seems that some of her church sisters saw the show.

"Mrs. Smart's daughter was on coast-to-coast TV and cooked naked greens!"

"What did you say?"

"Umhuhm, yes she did!"

"Where you think she picked that up?"

"Maybe she was raised like that."

"Umhuh, uumm, umm-umm!"

"It's a shame before the living justice, 'naked' greens."

"My, my, my . . ."

My choice of watermelon as the dessert on the show was controversial. Host Barbara Walters said, "Frankly," if it was up to her . . . she would not have chosen watermelon. Marie Brown, my editor, brought the watermelon to the studio. On her way, she ran into another black editor, who was horrified. "I wouldn't carry a watermelon in the streets for no author on no TV show!"

Scores of people called me up after the show to say that I should have chosen a menu that elevated "soul food."

Although *Vibration Cooking* was out of print for over a decade, I was constantly receiving letters from people who had "just discovered" the book. Sometimes they'd tell me how a certain recipe turned out, who they made it for, or who they were planning to make it for. Some people wanted to get in touch with their old friend "so-and-so" on page 83. . . . A lot of people said their copies had been stolen; where could they get another? Sadly, I would have to say, "It's out of print."

I am very happy that *Vibration Cooking* is back, for obvious reasons, and because a book is a great way to make friends. Take it from me, an autographed copy of your book will take you far. I've sent copies of *Vibration Cooking* to everyone I thought I might want to know, from politicians to movie stars.

When I announced that *Vibration Cooking* would be reissued, the Vibration Cookers started working on my nerves, again. My mother said, "Praise the Lord." . . . Now I could write more about her. My daughters wanted an update. "Please put in that we grew up." One is a great cook and one is a great specialty cook. Another person wanted me to take him out of the book and leave his recipe in. Somebody else wanted me to take her recipe out and leave her in. One person actually gave me an update; she now lives in Blah-blah, and was divorced from What's-his-name and living with So-and-so.

I love it!!!

In 1987, *Vibration Cooking* brought me an appearance on "Nightwatch," hosted by Charlie Rose. I was on with John Egerton. His book, *Southern Food: At Home, on the Road, in History*, is about the finest book on southern cooking that I've ever read. As they say, he gives it up! He acknowledges with relish, humor, and historical fact the contribution of African Americans to American cookery.

The "Nightwatch" producer asked me to bring some "Southern" dishes. I took cornbread, collard greens, and barbecued spareribs. I think the food was fingerlicking good because there were only a few crumbs of cornbread left at the end of the show.

Curious thing about the appearance was how many people saw it considering it comes on in the middle of the night. I'm telling you I had my fifteen minutes! I mean I got on the bus a few days later and the driver recognized me! "Hey Miss Soul Food." I started to go into my "Don't call it soul food" tirade but his smile was disarming, so I just smiled back.

The mass market edition of *Vibration Cooking* also got me a terrific spread in the *New York Times Home* section. Marian Burros interviewed me in South Carolina where I was renting a house. After she drove sixty-five miles way out in the country, I discovered that I didn't have the key to the house. It had been left at my Aunt Hattie's house, thirty miles away. Landlady and friend Freda Mitchell saved the day. I made lunch at her house next door. Marian didn't blink an eye. Thanks, Marian.

From 1987 to 1990, I did "The Book and the Cook," Philadelphia's culinary extravaganza where a cookbook author hooks up with a restaurant and creates a meal and signs books. Mama Rosa's restaurant in Germantown chose me two years in a row. The first year I participated in "The Book and the Cook" I met just about everybody who was anybody in the culinary world, from The Frugal Gourmet and Natalie Dupree to Bert Greene.

The most astounding change since the publication of *Vibration Cooking* has been in how people look at Geechee, or Gullah, culture. Back when the book first came out, people would ask me, "What's a geechee?" Last February, the Smithsonian sponsored a month of events celebrating Geechee or Gullah culture. I gave a lecture called "Growing Up Geechee."

One year, I went to a culinary symposium in Charleston, South Carolina, that was big fun and good eatin'. Charleston is a delicious town. It was the last time I saw Bert Greene, who wrote a glowing review of the mass market edition of *Vibration Cooking* for the *New York Daily News*.

In the years between the mass edition of *Vibration Cooking* and this One World edition, life for me has been comings and goings . . . people and places. I met Butterfly McQueen on a New York City bus, had lunch with Jimmy Carter at NPR, and met the Godfather of Soul, Mr. James Brown, in a Greek restaurant in Aiken, South Carolina. And I'm in the movies. Look for me—I play the hair-braider in Julie Dash's *Daughters of the Dust*. I went back to Paris for the first time in over a decade, I've been to the new South Africa and New Orleans.

I went to New Orleans for the first time ever in 1988. And headed straight for Dookey Chase's restaurant.

John Pinderhughes, author of *The Spirit of the Family*, was always singing the culinary praises of Leah Chase, "Leah can cook, you hear me. Leah can cook!" John didn't lie, Leah *can* cook!

And so can Austin Lee. His restaurant, Chez Helene, was the inspiration for the wonderful TV show "Frank's Place."

Truth be told, everyone in and from the Big Easy talks about food. They be serious. They sell food everywhere. I read about a woman who sold delicious and delectable morsels from the trunk of her car. Her enterprise was called Mama's Cadillac. She was so successful her son did the same thing. He called his business Junior's Pontiac.

In New Orleans, I became a culinary investigator, determined to find out if the city could live up to all that "New Orleans is the first city in the U.S. to consider cooking an art form, New Orleans is the culinary capital of the U.S." propaganda. I ate all over the city, jambalaya, crawfish pie, crawfish estouffe, dirty rice, red beans and rice, and every gumbo combo you can imagine. I ate everywhere from five-and-dime counters in the hood to elegant out-of-the-way places to tourist joints in the French Quarter.

I couldn't bust the Big Easy's reputation, but I'm not hardly go fix my mouth to join the "who makes the best gumbo" debate.

Early spring of 1991, Bob Tucker called me up and said he was a fan of *Vibration Cooking*, had the 1970 edition, and did I ever come to New Orleans and if I did, he and his wife, Gee, wanted to invite me over to eat. The call didn't seem strange to me. *Vibration Cooking* people were like that. In May, when I was in New Orleans for a public radio conference, I called him. "Come over, I'll cook gumbo for you," he insisted.

I explained that I was with colleagues. In true southern style Bob didn't miss a beat. "Bring 'em," he said.

Donna Limerick and Ben Davis went with me. Casually Ben asked, "How did you meet the Tuckers?"

"Well, I haven't yet. I've talked to him on the phone a lot. He knows me from my book," I replied.

"He knows you from your book? How do you know they aren't wackos or serial killers?"

"Trust me, I get good vibrations from him, trust me."

My vibrations were right on the money! Bob, his daughter Iam, and his right hand, Roxy, met us at the hotel, and by the end of the evening we were old friends. The dinner was too good— scrumptious. As Paul Lawrence Dunbar said in his poem "The Party," "I can't tell you all we had, you oughta have been there." The pièce de la résistance was a dish Bob called Chicken à la

Vertamae. When they brought it out, you could have knocked me over with a chicken feather.

*   *   *   *

. . . I got to tell you that reading a book originally written in 1970 again in 1991 was rough. *Vibration Cooking or The Travel Notes of a Geechee Girl* made me pause. For over a month, I could not read more than a few pages at a time. It was too "this is your life Vertamae . . . these are your peoples." So many peoples, so many relationships, so much food and so many friends.

I have and have had some great friends. Reading *Vibration Cooking* again made me want to get in touch with the living and weep for the dead.

My dear friend Arrone, whom I met all those years ago on the ss *Rotterdamm* when I sailed to Europe in search of the bohemians, is gone. Orde Coombs, Alfredo Viazzi, Eleanor Munson, Ellis Haizlip, Bill Gunn, Charles Sanders, Sam Floyd, Bernard Haskell, Bill Neal, Romare Bearden, Miguel Pinero and Jimmy have all gone.

Jimmy, James Arthur Baldwin. His funeral was the best home-going service, the most spectacular farewell I have ever witnessed or heard about. It was held in the Cathedral of St. John the Divine. Between the incense and the drums of Baabatunde Olatunji I thought I would faint and I almost did when at the end Jimmy sang "Precious Lord, Take My Hand."

The funeral was so awesome. I told my friends, "Listen up. If you don't think you can have a funeral like Jimmy's, keep your Black ass alive." Read Clyde Taylor who wrote a moving piece about it in *James Baldwin, The Legacy.*

I'm so proud of my friends in the creative community who have kept the faith, and kept on doing what they do. I bust with pride and actually scream and holler when I see them on the screen or TV. I always buy their books. I know how annoyed I feel when somebody asks me to "give" them a book.

I even bought a TV crossword overpriced magazine because Anna Maria Horsford was on the cover. Anna is one of the stars of "Amen." I first met her when she was a producer of "Soul with Ellis" for PBS.

"Soul" had vision. I was in Cleveland, Ohio, for a *Vibration Cooking or The Travel Notes of a Geechee Girl* book party, hosted by a Black women's club. The sisters knew how to treat you. There was a lovely dinner and afterwards the son of one of the members entertained us with his magic tricks. He was very funny, and I came back and told Anna Horsford, "You gotta book this kid. He's good." Anna said, "OK, what's his name?" "Arsenio Hall, and he's going to be a star."

The last time I saw Miguel Pinero was at a dinner party in his honor at the Barakas' home in Newark. Amina and Amiri give some dinner parties. I've heard people admit, "I can't stand Baraka's politics but I love his parties." The Barakas always have dancing parties, with poetry readings, often live music, and sho nuff live guests. And you can count on having lots of good good food. Amina can cook. Her mama Ruth can cook. Her sister Sheila can cook, and when they all cook for a party, just shut your mouth wide open.

There are some friends whom I suspect invite me over just to cook. They claim they want to see me so badly and could I come over and could they borrow my big cast-iron skillet or my big stock pot and when I get there they are so intimidated by such a big black cast-iron skillet could I fix the chicken since it's my pot! And since it's such a big pot and we'll have too much just for us, let's invite some people over . . . Now they think they're exploiting me, but they really aren't. I like the challenge of a strange kitchen, I like it when folks say "That was so good." In the book *I Dream a World*, Leontyne Price says, "I love nothing better than hearing my voice." Well, I likes eating food I cooked.

I've said it before and will say it again: Write a cookbook and you'll never be lonely.

When people ask what are the most important changes in my life since the mass market edition of *Vibration Cooking*, I say life and death.

On April 21, 1988, my grandson Oscar Brown IV was born to my youngest daughter Chandra and her husband Oscar Brown III, who also goes by the name of Bobo. I have to stop right here and say that during the '60s Oscar Brown, Jr.'s song "Brown Baby" was my children's cradle song. Now I sing the song to a real brown baby.

To make a long and wonderful birthing story short, I'll just tell you that I was in the delivery room when Oscar was born.

Originally Chandra was going to the birthing center, but due to a complication she was sent to the hospital. We brought our "birthing room" attitudes with us. I don't know nothing 'bout birthing no babies, but I tried not to let it show. The doctor spoke to me and I thought he said "You look like a painter." With my hands on my hips and a toss of my dreadlocks I set him straight, "I'm not a painter, I'm a writer." A few minutes later, Oscar was born and I was out.

The nurses were ready with the smelling salts or whatever it is they give you. It turns out, the doctor had said "You look like a fainter." I recovered and did my assignment, to count the fingers and toes. Oscar was beautiful. My heart filled with a love I have never known.

In April 1991, my mother died at the age of eighty-nine in South Carolina. She suffered a stroke last summer and never really recovered. Watching her deteriorate those last months broke my heart.

I will treasure the last conversations we had before her mind slipped away. She stopped eating, said she couldn't stand the hospital food. The doctors, nurses, family, and I all pleaded with her to eat.

"Mama," I said, "please eat. They say you'll die less you eat."

She looked at me, smiled her gap-toothed smile and said in that singsong, melodic voice, "I don't want their food. I guess your seasoning done spoiled me."

People tell me that time heals all wounds. Maybe so, but time passes and memory stays. I miss Mama so much. At the funeral Kali was very sick. We thought it was grief and stress. She was pregnant. On the full moon of November 22, here comes Charlotte Rose Grosvenor-Jeffries, with big ruby red lips and long long fingers, just like mama . . .

For the record, the grandmother did not faint this time.

Vertamae
New York City
October 1991

INDEX OF RECIPES